ENDORSEMENTS

"Refreshingly vulnerable, witty and wise. *Waiting for Jack* feels like a conversation with your best friend over coffee. With an honest approach and take action message, Kristen Moeller motivates readers to make it happen. This book is a special gift and thank you Kristen for writing it!"

Robyn Spizman, New York Times Bestselling Author, Creator of TheGiftionary.com and well-known media personality
www.robynspizman.com

"*Waiting for Jack* will give anyone an intimate view into genuine healing and growth. Kristen Moeller is a compassionate healer with an enormous gift for communication."

Janet Attwood, author of the New York Times Bestseller
. *The Passion Test*
www.thepassiontest.com

"*Waiting for Jack* is a powerful story of transformation under the most challenging of circumstances. Kristen will open your eyes to a whole new world of possibility and allow you to see your own life in a new way. Incredibly inspiring *and* informative. It's a must-read."

Bob Doyle, featured teacher in *The Secret*
www.wealthbeyondreason.com

"I am so appreciative of Kristen's honesty and eye-opening journey to living now instead of in fear of what might be. *Waiting for Jack* poses questions we should all ask ourselves and be brave enough to hear the answers!"

Emme, supermodel, television personality, and women's advocate
www.emmestyle.com

"Kristen Moeller has written a powerful guide for discovering the true meaning of trust. She invites us to release fear and open to the infinite possibilities of living fully."

Cynthia James, author of *What Will Set You Free* and
Transformational specialist
www.whatwillsetyoufree.com

"Kristen's simply and beautifully described self-journey inspires a profound, quiet, deeply central truth about who we are and how to embrace our 'gift.' Living up to her mission—'fiercely disrupting the ordinary'—Kristen takes readers on our own deeply personal journey of realization ... that in this very moment, we are more than we could ever hope to need, want, or be in this life. She expresses with exquisite clarity not only the richness that is available to each of us if we only choose to consciously create our own life each day, but offers a clear recipe for achieving extraordinary meaning and fulfillment. Be prepared to feel inspired, engage with your true passions, and find new ways to live your humanity beginning today."

Gary Goldstein, movie producer (*Pretty Woman*),
author, speaker, and coach
www.garywgoldstein.com

"*Waiting for Jack* delivers a heartfelt and inspiring message as well as a concrete action plan to get off the sidelines of your life and uncover your inner power. Kristen brings her nineteen years in the field of personal development as well as her unique personal experience to provide readers a journey back to themselves—where they discover they don't have to "wait for Jack"—or, anything else for that matter, outside themselves."

Pat Burns, author of *Grandparents Rock*
www.grandparentsrock.com

"What are you waiting for? Stop letting life pass you by! Kristen shows us how to stop waiting and start living *now!* Life is a moment-to-moment creation. Rather than waiting for the perfect moment, Kristen teaches us how to create it. *Waiting for Jack* will give you the tools to live an inspired, empowered, and fulfilling life now!"

Laura Duksta, author of the New York Times Bestseller
I Love You More
www.LauraDuksta.com

"In *Waiting for Jack,* Kristen eloquently demonstrates how to become responsible for all areas of our life, including our relationship to money. So often, people don't get that wealth is a spiritual concept and that money is a byproduct of value creation. It's crucial to learn how to take responsibility for your life and do it in a way that is consistent with who you are from a spiritual perspective."

Garrett B. Gunderson, author of *Killing Sacred Cows*
www.killingsacredcows.com

"Kristen Moeller's ability to tap into one of the great longings of human-kind—that somehow what we've got now is never enough—is riveting. I love her courage in tackling this big subject, the intimacy of her voice (she's been there and we know it!), and her far-reaching wisdom. Thanks, Kristen, for putting our longing into words and helping us navigate our way through it. I'm done 'waiting'!"

Suzanne Falter-Barns, author of *How Much Joy Can You Stand*
www.howmuchjoy.com

"*Waiting for Jack* is a refreshing take on personal development where you can let go of the constant need for 'development' and find peace in knowing that where you are is exactly where you need to be. Kristen's stories are so brazenly honest that they touch you to the core and unveil the pieces of your life that you have been hiding from or neglecting to face. Reading this book, you will feel normal, connected, loved and empowered to live an extraordinary life.

> Debra Berndt, author of *Let Love In: How to Open Your Heart and Mind to Attract Your Ideal Partner*
> www.attractreallove.com

"Kristen Moeller is an amazing life coach who will "radically" change your life. Her book *Waiting for Jack* is full of wisdom, understanding, clarity, and practical action steps. As you read this book, you will remember that you are perfection *right now*. No need to "wait" to live your life; create your life right now! *Waiting for Jack* is a masterpiece!!"

> Andrea Joy Cohen, MD, physician, keynote speaker, Bestselling author of *A Blessing in Disguise-39 Life Lessons from Today's Greatest Teachers,* Penguin www.drandreajoycohen.com

"Kristen Moeller casts light on our ordinary perspective and makes a whole new perspective possible. By sharing her trials and errors, she embraces her extraordinary humanity and allows us to do the same. *Waiting for Jack* shows us our relentless and human journey of searching for an elusive destination when in fact we have already arrived. Kristen Moeller provides us with the one answer we forget was there all along—we have all the tools we need to build any life we desire."

> Kenneth L. Weiner, M.D., Cofounder and Medical Director of the Eating Recovery Center, Denver, Colorado
> www.eatingrecoverycenter.com

WAITING FOR JACK

Confessions of a Self-Help Junkie
How to Stop Waiting and Start Living Your Life

KRISTEN MOELLER

New York

Waiting for Jack
Confessions of a Self-Help Junkie
How To Stop Waiting and Start Living Your Life

Cover Design by: Johnson2Design   www.Johnson2Design.com
                                     megan@Johnson2Design.com

Scripture taken from the Holy Bible: International Standard Version® Release 2.0. Copyright © 1996-2009 by the ISV Foundation. Used by permission of Davidson Press, LLC. ALL RIGHTS RESERVED INTERNATIONALLY.

Original artwork provided by Dorothy C. Westby
For information about the artist please contact her at dcw@westbystudios.com
                                     www.westbystudios.com

ISBN 978-1-60037-725-9

Library of Congress Control Number: 2009941838

Morgan James Publishing
1225 Franklin Ave., STE 325
Garden City, NY 11530-1693
Toll Free 800-485-4943
www.MorganJamesPublishing.com

In an effort to support local communities, raise awareness and funds, Morgan James Publishing donates one percent of all book sales for the life of each book to Habitat for Humanity. Get involved today, visit **www.HelpHabitatForHumanity.org.**

DEDICATION

In honor and memory of my first mentor, Susan Hansen, whose voice I can still hear saying "I am blown away, thrilled to death to be alive." Your laughter was infectious. Your light shined brightly. Sadly for us, you left this earth sooner than anyone was ready to let you go. You shared your love, light, and joy with hundreds of people whose lives you touched.

Thank you for being one of my greatest teachers.

CONTENTS

FOREWORD

I first met Kristen Moeller while leading a workshop in Denver, Colorado. I had no idea at the time that our meeting would initiate a journey for Kristen, taking on a major life challenge and ultimately inspiring her to write this book. *Waiting for Jack* is the book you've been waiting for, and oddly enough, it is the impetus to stop waiting and start living.

The story actually begins with Kristen waiting to hear from me, Jack. As she observes herself waiting for my response to her e-mails, she seizes the opportunity to look at all the areas of her life where she, perhaps unwittingly, is waiting instead of living. Of course, it seems our dilemma as humans is to wait for an externally derived solution to our problems. We seem compulsive in our efforts to seek answers, comfort, and direction from "out there." We look to others for guidance and hope for a lightning bolt of understanding, expecting an authority outside ourselves—perhaps a book, a teacher like myself, or a spiritual belief—to tell us what to do and how to do it so we might finally be happy, healthy, and wealthy.

In this book, Kristen Moeller asks, "Why wait?"

With a wonderfully personal and engaging style, Kristen offers her intimate life story, providing a raw and powerful account of her personal struggles. With every chapter, she demonstrates her rare courage and willingness to be completely authentic while unflinchingly dismantling her life to see all the places where she has passively waited for something to change. She writes with the commitment to act, fiercely embracing her humanity so that the rest of us might do the same.

In each chapter we have the opportunity to review our own journey, watch where we are stopped, where we are unresolved and stuck in our lives. Kristen directs us to find our own "inner Jack" by asking us to consider questions, such as:

Where do you find yourself thinking you are not enough?
Do you belong to your body, or does your body belong to you?
Are you waiting for enough money, a better romantic relationship?
How are you limiting your experience of life?
And perhaps most importantly, can you embrace what you don't know?

By the end of this book and your personal exploration, you will see where you wait for life to begin. You will see that all the answers you need come from within. You will learn to stop hiding your magnificence and stop jacking around. You will become, as Kristen proclaims, "a fierce disruption of the ordinary!"

—Jack Canfield
Co-author, *Chicken Soup for the Soul* and *The Success Principles*

Confessions of a Self-Help Junkie

Wisdom is to see that there is nothing to search for.
From *Everyday Zen* by Charlotte Joko Beck

The first step is to admit there is a problem. So here goes … my name is Kristen and I am addicted to the eternal search for self-improvement. To put it more bluntly, I am a self-help junkie. I didn't intend to be. As you will learn, I began this path of seeking personal growth innocently enough, but passion turned to obsession, and later, a driving compulsion, pulling me toward a destination I couldn't reach.

I was convinced there was a rule book for life *and* that I didn't have it. Like many addictions, it wasn't always a negative experience. And in this case, it hasn't been hugely destructive, *unless* you define destructive as never allowing yourself to arrive. Never quite getting there, never really relaxing. Not completely settling in …

So on that life-altering day when I caught myself waiting for Jack, I wondered …

> When did self-help become synonymous with "there's something wrong with me"? Or with anyone?
>
> How did it become about the eternal search for something, a search outside the self?
>
> Why did it become about needing the perfect teacher, book, course or practice?

How did it become about something out there on
the horizon?

When did it become a dirty word?

To be clear, there is nothing inherently wrong with self-help. Many
of us wouldn't be where we are today if we hadn't taken this journey.
Additionally, I have found that most people who are drawn to self-help
have a huge commitment to make a difference in the world.

The root of the "problem" lies in our relationship to it, our bottomless
quest to be someone, something or somewhere other than we are, our
endless seeking, searching—and waiting. The type of waiting that
disguises itself in many clever ways, hiding quietly in the nuances of
life or sometimes brazenly and in our face.

I became determined to illuminate these patterns for myself and
others like me who are stuck on the self-help treadmill. Those who
are determined to find the answers but on a deep level, a level often
kept hidden beneath awareness, remain unsatisfied. For those who are
starving in the midst of plenty, this *is* what self-help has become.

I declared that it's time to reinvent our relationship to self-help. And I
knew I couldn't do it alone.

My Invitation for You

I invite you to join me on this journey; to grapple with this inquiry;
to explore our bottomless quest for improvement. I offer you my own
"confessions." And when I say confessions I mean both the lessons
learned and the wisdom gained along the way. I include stories
of others who have disrupted their ordinary patterns of endlessly
searching and waiting—people who have created what they want in
life by discovering their unique expression as they learn to embrace the
ever-present human condition. Some of these examples are extreme.
You may not think you can relate, but extreme examples frequently

illustrate that which remains subtle within us. As you read, consider looking for the similarities. Reflect where, in your own life, you might be waiting or searching outside yourself for answers. Contemplate decisions you have made about yourself and the world which might have been useful at the time but are no longer serving you. See if you have become a self-help junkie.

I am certainly not saying that by reading this book you will *never* fall into these patterns again. I am not claiming you will never wait again. Or that you will always remember who you are. The tragic fate of the human condition is to forget constantly. We have what is referred to in twelve-step programs as a "built in forgetter." My purpose in writing this book is for us to spend more time remembering.

In part one, *Body,* I share how I became a seeker, not a finder. I illustrate how we make decisions throughout our lives that form (and limit) who we become. I demonstrate what is possible when we look at our lives with a new perspective.

In part two, *Mind,* each chapter covers specific areas of life where you may wait: career and purpose, love and relationships, money and spending, home and places, and health and illness. You will have the opportunity to uncover your patterns of waiting, how and where you wait, and for what or whom.

In part three, *Spirit,* I take a deeper look at why we are the way we are. You will be left with compassion for your humanity and an invitation to be a fierce disruption of the ordinary in your own life and the world—*whatever that means to you.*

Scattered throughout the book, I share "practices" that I have learned and incorporated over the years. I use these practices to wake myself up when I slide into the trap of waiting and searching. Each chapter concludes with explorations called "What Are You Waiting For?" designed to deepen the inquiry. Ponder and play with each of these. Be willing to see something you haven't noticed before. Consider keeping a journal as you read to record your insights.

In the end, I invite you to discover that who you are *is* who you want to be. And maybe, together we can alter the status quo. We can disrupt our ordinary. We can reinvent our relationship to self-help *and* we can remember who we are.

PART ONE:

BODY

Mistakes are the portals of discovery—James Joyce

1

WAITING FOR JACK

Get busy living or get busy dying.
Morgan Freeman as Red in
The Shawshank Redemption

The first time I met Jack, I ripped a hundred-dollar bill out of his hand.

On a cold winter day, I waited in line to see one of my heroes, Jack Canfield, the co-author of the best-selling *Chicken Soup for the Soul* series. He was speaking at Mile High Church in Denver to a packed house and a sold out show. Determined to get the best seats possible, I persuaded my dear friend Lainie to accompany me in line, in spite of the biting February rain. Nestling as close as possible to the building, under the overhang, we dined on our takeout burritos until two hours later when they finally opened the door. I was determined!

Jack's topic for the event was his book, *The Success Principles: How to Get from Where You Are to Where You Want to Be*. Where I wanted to be was a version of what Jack had become—an author, a national speaker, an inspiration to thousands of people. He was the whole package—successful, charming, kind, and thoughtful—a visionary for what is possible in the world. I thought, "If I can get to know him, I will become *that.*"

When I saw the opportunity, I grabbed it. Literally. During his presentation, Jack reached for his wallet, pulled out a hundred-dollar bill, and said, "Who wants this?" Hands shot up in the audience;

people leaned forward to see whom Jack would choose. But I leapt up, ran up the stairs to the stage, and grabbed the bill from his hand. As I was launching myself in the air, all sorts of thoughts ran through my mind: "Was I about to be humiliated in front of 800 people? Would they call security and haul me from the stage?" But my desire for bold action was louder than any of the other voices of doubt.

As I plucked the bill from his hand, Jack turned to me and said, "Yes! That's it! We can't wait around for the opportunities to come to us. We must take *action* to create what we say we want!"

After his talk, again I waited in line to meet Jack (formally, this time!) and boldly asked for his personal e-mail address. I was thrilled when he gave it to me. Over the next several months I sent him lengthy e-mails sharing my vision, dreams, and what I was trying to create. He kindly e-mailed back one-liners of encouragement such as, "Keep thinking and playing bigger; it's much more fun that way. Love, Jack." After a few months, my inspiration faded, I filled my life with other things, and I stopped e-mailing Jack.

A year later, my dreams had grown stale. I had this idea if I got back in touch with Jack, he might just provide the perfect, inspiring nudge I needed. I was looking for *something* that would spur me into action, like a giant arrow that would show me the way and lead me in the right direction.

I e-mailed Jack; then a few days later, I e-mailed him again. I got no response. Distressed, I wondered, "What if I never hear from him again? What if I have blown this important connection?"

In the midst of a family gathering, I sneaked away to check my e-mail— for the fifth time in fifteen minutes …

Suddenly I woke up!

What was I doing?

Even after all these years of growth and development—my extensive training and experience—*I was waiting!*

This time, I was waiting for Jack.

I've repeatedly heard we have only this one precious life. We need to go for the gusto, get off the sidelines, and play the game! In books, seminars, and various disciplines I've studied and experienced, the underlying message is always the same: *All we have is now.* And yet here I was *waiting* for something special to happen *outside* of me—searching for something or someone to make me feel inspired again.

When I looked further, I didn't like what I saw. Not only was I waiting, I was *impatiently* waiting for Jack. I was compulsively checking my e-mail, hoping my scrutiny would compel him to write me back. I was preoccupied, thinking *he* was the answer—that somehow he could provide what I (mistakenly) thought I was missing. I was putting my life on hold instead of getting out there in the world and creating what I said I want to create.

Then I realized, "If I am *still* waiting, then others must be too." I recalled that day in Denver. Many of the people in the audience were probably sitting in their chairs thinking, "I want that hundred-dollar bill!" They were, as Jack had pointed out, waiting. I recalled my recent trip to the supermarket where I glanced at magazine headlines that seemed to scream out, "Buy me and I'll change your life! The answer is in here—on my glossy pages!" If we believe the headlines, we clearly lack *something.* We have forgotten where the answers truly are.

An Oliver Wendell Holmes quote ran through my mind: "Many people die with their music still in them." He goes on to say, "Why is this so? Too often it is because they are always getting ready to live. Before they know it, time runs out." In that moment, I knew I needed to do something about all of this waiting—and I was inspired to write this book.

The Status Quo

For many of us, patterns of waiting and searching begin in childhood. Each year as Christmas approached, I could barely sleep. I longed not only for the magic of *that* morning—the fresh snow and twinkling lights on the tree—but also for *that* particular present. The thing I felt I had to possess that I hoped would make me feel complete. The Barbie doll, the miniskirt—whatever it happened to be that year. As I got older, I discovered boys and waited for my first kiss, my first love. Surely, when he arrived I would be whole; I would be the true me. Then I waited by the phone for *him* to call.

Convinced the real excitement of life was just around the corner, I waited to earn the freedom of my driver's license. Then I waited to graduate high school, as surely my "real" life would begin in college. On and on it went.

Waiting for what comes next has become our method of relating to the world, our learned way of being. We wait with the intention of *my life will be better when* …We wait to earn more money, to have less debt, to get married (or to get divorced), to have children, to retire. Many of us even wait to become spiritually enlightened! We wait for the next teacher, guru, or therapist; he or she will finally explain the meaning of life. We anticipate that the new experience or the next seminar or retreat will provide answers. We wait for recognition, to be discovered, to feel safe, to get it right. We wait to feel inspired (one of my personal favorites). We wait until our affairs are in order, our eggs are in different baskets, our ducks are in a row. We wait because when that thing arrives or happens, we will be fine, *then* we will be happy.

This type of waiting is distinct from being patient. As it is said, patience is a virtue. When we are patient, we are at ease. We freely allow ourselves to trust the process. We consciously allow life to unfold. However, when we wait, we put our life on hold. We become trapped in our impatience and turmoil. We define ourselves by that thing or experience that is supposed to change it all and make it better. We are not present to life, and we lose sight of who we really are.

Paradoxically, we wait and try to get somewhere at the same time—and that *somewhere* is anywhere but here, in the moment, in the now. We believe when we get *there* or have *that,* we will possess eternal happiness. We look for the magic pill. But what if we've already swallowed it? What if we were born with it? What if we *are* it?

To Seek is Human

Ships at a distance have every man's wish on board. For some they come in with the tide. For others they sail forever on the horizon, never out of sight, never landing until the Watcher turns his eyes away in resignation, his dreams mocked to death by Time. That is the life of men.
Zora Neale Hurston

It has been said the journey within is the most important journey of all. Many of us follow a path, searching for meaning—for something bigger. Although this is a worthwhile endeavor, do we search at the expense of finding?

We incessantly seek, convinced the next big *thing* will finally give us the answer that will make everything all right. We remain seduced by a distant destination, sailing with one eye always on the horizon, forgetting that the destination might just be a mirage.

Our lucrative and enormous self-help industry actually depends upon us seeking endlessly, walking a path without arriving at that elusive destination—enlightenment. Type "self-help" into the search function at Amazon.com, and you will find more than 172,000 book titles alone. Often we read these books without taking the necessary action that will allow us to create the transformation we want. We might even think they contain "the answer," yet these books will not change us. Only *we* can take the action that will create the transformation we seek.

Many of us are actually addicted to self-improvement. Some, like me, are admitted self-help junkies! The common theme is we never quite settle in. We keep going and going, peeling back more and more layers of the proverbial onion, hoping one day we will find the truth about life and ourselves. One day we will arrive and everything will make sense. We will finally be okay. We will be "fixed."

Not only do we perpetually seek, we act as though we have all the time in the world to get there. In truth, we live in a physical body and in a physical world—our clocks are ticking. Tragically, many of us live our entire lives without fulfilling our dreams. Why is this?

We have a case of what is called "the human condition." In her book *Eat, Pray, Love*, Elizabeth Gilbert describes the human condition as "the heartbreaking inability to sustain contentment." We seem to have a basic dissatisfaction with *what is*. We want things, people, places, and ourselves—in short, *our lives*—to be different. And we want a quick fix. We want it all now. So we search endlessly, look outside ourselves relentlessly, *and we wait*. We are busy searching, wanting, hoping, and praying, but we aren't living; living our lives *as if*, as if we have arrived, as if we are enough.

> What if we are enough and have enough, right now, as we are?

> What if, instead of changing how we are, how we look, or what we do, we start by changing our perspective?

> What if we could see ourselves and the world differently—with more compassion and less criticism?

> What if we chose growth for its own sake—from the joy of discovery—and not from a sense of lack?

> What if we realized there was nothing to wait for?

BECOMING A FIERCE DISRUPTION OF THE ORDINARY

When I realized I was waiting for Jack, I declared that I would disrupt the status quo, the ordinariness of waiting. I declared an end to my "search addiction" and that I would quit gazing outward for answers. I allowed myself to imagine a whole planet of people so fulfilled that the "self-help" industry proved unnecessary and actually disappeared—a planet of people who already understood that they are okay as they are, with their flaws, their social standing, their level of popularity, the amount of money they have in the bank, and their level of spiritual enlightenment. That would be extraordinary. We could turn our attention away from our external wandering and focus on what is essential, whether it's living in the present moment, making a difference in the world, or cleaning the refrigerator. The extraordinary thing would be that we get to choose. If we wanted to search, we could search. If we wanted to wait, we could wait. But we could do it from a place of knowing that we are whole and complete. Now *that* would be a fierce disruption of our ordinary!

The status quo is to live an ordinary life. There is nothing wrong with that. Ordinary isn't bad and extraordinary isn't good. However, ordinary can be limiting, and many of us *say* we want more.

Some of the "ordinary" patterns we can fall into are:

Waiting (and putting our lives on hold).

Looking outside ourselves for answers.

Allowing self-doubt to get in the way of going after what we want.

Lacking respect for ourselves and others.

Forgetting our power.

Losing sight of who we really are.

Giving up.

Constantly being in a hurry.

Forgetting to appreciate the simple things.

Disrupting the ordinary can be expressed in countless ways. By being a better friend, being a more supportive co-worker, or running for the president of the United States. By writing a book, picking up litter, or saying "thank you." By trying to solve world hunger, kissing your grandmother, or remembering to take out the trash.

I am *not* here to tell you what being a fierce disruption of the ordinary should look like for you. You get to decide that. I invite you to begin the inquiry.

Imagine once upon a time you knew you were perfect.
At some point you forgot.
You started trying to get somewhere.
You were waiting for your life to start. You looked outside yourself for
*   the answers.*
You forgot you already had all of the answers.
You lost sight of your dreams or told yourself you didn't have any.
You stopped living your life fully. You kept searching but never finding.
You settled for a life of fixing yourself.
Now you can stop ...

WHAT ARE YOU WAITING FOR?

1. Do you incessantly search and never settle in?
2. Are you a self-help junkie?
3. What are *you* waiting for? For instance, are you waiting for happiness, safety, money or a relationship?
4. What does a disruption of the ordinary mean to you?
5. What have you forgotten about who you really are?

*Now I take you back to my story of how
I became a seeker and not a finder ...*

2
JACK SPRAT COULD EAT NO FAT

*There are three great mysteries of nature: Air to the
bird, water to the fish, and man to himself.*
Hindu proverb

S tanding ankle-deep in a pool of vomit in the girls' bathroom of my college dorm, I wondered, "How did I get here? How did I go from the Dolly Parton Diet to *this?*"

While some of my classmates were clear about their goals for college and actually attended classes and studied for exams, I tried to find the safest places to throw up after binging. The showers were loud and steamy enough to hide the sounds and smells, and I could get clean as the water washed away the mess.

Later in my dorm room, I glanced out the window at the clear Boulder sky with a stabbing pain of awareness: I was missing my life. I felt trapped and longed for something else. I continually promised myself, "Tomorrow, it will be different. Tomorrow, I will start living my life. I will do all those things you are supposed to do in Colorado. I will live the outdoor lifestyle, hike, camp, or just be outside. I *will* stop this disgusting behavior. Tomorrow—because today is lost." I hid in my room and wondered, "When did my life become about finding the next bathroom? When did I start comparing myself to others and coming up short? When did I decide I needed to be perfect?"

EARLY DECISIONS

> Small things can set us off—tiny incidents that matter to no one else but loom large in our minds. We latch onto them, magnify them, and they become indelible, forming who we become. Even though these events may have occurred long ago, we get messages, learn lessons, and make decisions that impact our feelings, thinking, and behavior. When we make these formative decisions, we are not always aware that we alter the course of our lives.

From this vantage point, looking back on my early life, I can clearly see how I allowed external events to shape and define me. With each life challenge, I made a decision about myself, building a perception that led to my self-destructive behavior.

One of these early pivotal moments occurred for me in the third grade as my class took turns reading aloud. When it was my turn, my proud moment in my new class, I began reading enthusiastically, but faltered at the point in the book where it said, "Chicago is known as the Windy City." Plowing onward, I read, *"Chick*-a-go is known …" The entire room erupted in laughter, and my face became red hot. I plopped down in complete humiliation. At that moment I made a critical decision: I never wanted to feel that way again! Therefore, I would never again speak in class without *knowing* the answer. My embarrassment was overwhelming. Even if I was sure I knew the answer, I would remain silent anyway. This behavior followed me throughout my life, even in graduate school where I earned straight As.

Soon after, another significant event occurred that reinforced my self-doubt. My mother dropped me off at a classmate's birthday party, and as I watched her car pull out of the driveway, I had a sickening realization—this was a boy's birthday party. I had brought a beautifully wrapped present for a *girl*. Instead of an action figure, the birthday boy was about to receive a purple fairy doll.

I mechanically ate pizza and birthday cake while dreading the moment he opened his presents. I cast around for ideas to hide or escape, but I was trapped, watching him slowly unwrap his gifts one by one. I knew I would soon be found out, and I pictured the other kids turning to look at me and laughing. I don't recall the boy actually opening his present. I was consumed by worry—I only remember *waiting* for something to happen.

FAILING TO GET IT RIGHT

My fear of judgment grew, and I developed creative ways to avoid any possible embarrassment. I took riding lessons at a local stable. I loved horses, and even pretended to be one, galloping around and eating grass. But every week when we drove to the stable, I became increasingly anxious. My stomach ached. I wanted to escape.

One day was particularly stressful. I knew we were going to practice jumping in the indoor arena and people would *watch*. During the drive, I saw the familiar scenery pass by the window and felt my fear grow as we got closer. I desperately considered ways to avoid having to jump. Had my mom been driving, I could pretend to be sick and she would let me off the hook. As it was, a friend's mom was behind the wheel. I suffered in agonizing silence.

When we arrived at the arena, we began trotting our horses to warm them up. I came up with the only plan I could think of to get away from the impending scrutiny—I fell off my horse and pretended to have hurt my finger. I cleverly wrapped it in a band-aid, using a bobby pin as a splint. Scrutiny turned to sympathy, and I felt enormous relief. Eureka! Hurting myself, I realized, was not only a way to get attention, but it was a way out of things I was afraid to do.

At age eight, another event occurred that shattered my world. My parents sat down with my brother, Rob and me to tell us our father was moving out. I felt the earth shift—I had seen no signs this was coming!

I thought we were the *perfect* family. My dad moved to an apartment in Boston. Mom, Rob and I moved to the dream house my parents had just finished building together. My eight-year-old brain tried to make sense of what was happening. I wondered, "Was it my fault? Was I not a good enough kid? If I had only known, could I have prevented the split?" The only logical conclusion I could come up with was that I clearly lacked *something*.

Mark Epstein writes in his book, *Going on Being,* "When awareness is hijacked early in life by the need to react to or manage environmental insufficiencies, this hijacking leaves holes in a person's sense of self." What Epstein means is that our sense of self is taken over, even lost, which leaves us believing we have a "hole" or a void. Prior to the hijacking, everything *seems* fine. Then something happens where we are embarrassed or hurt or at a loss, and there is that "uh-oh" moment. Usually we interpret this negatively, as in "something is wrong with me," and that is the metaphorical "hole" in our self. We then develop ways of compensating and interacting with the world (like waiting). These protective mechanisms may serve us initially, but later they keep us trapped. For some, self-image and esteem suffers, and feelings of self-doubt and of not being good enough become entrenched.

After our parents separated, we spent Wednesday evenings and every other weekend with Dad. After our visits, Dad tucked us each into bed and read a story before heading back to Boston. I desperately wanted him to stay and clutched tightly to his arm. Each time, as I listened to the gravel crunching under his tires when he pulled out of the driveway, I silently declared: "I will *never* be left again."

Of course, in the normal course of life, people come and go—sometimes by choice, sometimes unexpectedly through uncontrollable events. A series of such events began when I was eleven. First my aunt died in a motorcycle accident on a sunny, New England autumn day. As she drove past Walden Pond she rounded the corner too wide and was hit by a truck approaching from the other direction. I was devastated. Then my maternal grandmother was dying of cancer, and halfway through the school year we moved to Fort Lauderdale, Florida, where my grandmother lived.

Instead of dealing with my own feelings of loss (the hole in myself), I focused on my dread and fear about the move, which required making new friends and starting over. I had waited so long to be an upperclassman in the seventh grade. Fortunately, in Florida I discovered something miraculous: Mickey's Big Mouth Beer. My new friends and I could easily purchase it at a nearby gas station. I strolled home guzzling beer and feeling bigger than life. My sadness and self-doubt temporarily disappeared. Here was a new kind of confidence that came with a sense of freedom—this felt good! For the moment, my life looked rosy.

Even with this new way to avoid my angst, I longed for my old life and friends in Massachusetts. My mom wanted us to stay. My father wanted us with him. I felt conflicted and didn't know how to choose between my parents. Finally a compromise was reached. I would return to Florida for my last two years of high school, and my brother and I moved back to Massachusetts.

With every move I tried hard to fit in. Starting at each new school, I had to determine the perfect clothes to wear. This time I thought I had the advantage—I purchased the tight, oh-so-cute designer jeans, meticulously ironed and cuffed, considered *haute couture* in Florida.

Wrong, wrong, wrong! As it turned out, these Massachusetts girls wore alligator shirts and chinos. It seemed the more shirts you layered, the higher your status. Sandy was clearly the coolest with three raised collars under her pinstriped, button-down shirt. This trend was termed "preppy." My style was referred to as "tacky." I felt completely humiliated again. Now I *knew* I would never get it right.

MY SOLUTIONS

To my disappointment, it was much more difficult for a thirteen-year-old to buy alcohol in my small New England town than in "Fort Liquordale." Consequently, my friends and I found it necessary to rely upon an older schoolmate who served as both babysitter and alcohol distributor.

On a weekend trip to the beach hosted by my unsuspecting father, four of us smuggled a newly acquired case of Bud hidden deep in our duffel bags, each can carefully wrapped in an article of clothing. That evening we filled our pockets with the cans and ran down to the beach. We rolled around in the sand, laughed, and sang songs. Again my troubles disappeared. I drank eight in a row and vomited all night. What a blast!

I began to really love alcohol. It provided benefits I had not cultivated internally. It eased my intolerable anxiety and gave me access to a social niche. I no longer felt like an outsider. I could join a group of people with similar avoidance practices, drop my inhibitions, have fun, and finally *relax*.

Upon my promised return to live with mom in Florida, I delighted in the discovery of recreational drugs. Some mornings we snorted coke in the senior parking lot. Once we had a party during lunch hour at the drug dealer's house. I recall the plastic baggie being passed my way and plunging my straw deep inside the white powder, inhaling so much I hyperventilated. This was *so cool.*

As cool as I felt, the realities of life could not be ignored entirely. At home, life wasn't great. My mother drank to cope with her losses, and both she and my brother always seemed sad. I craved support and understanding and had no idea how to get it. I felt completely, utterly alone. I once told my father, "I wish something was wrong with me so people would pay attention to me."

SOMETHING "WRONG" WITH ME

If you saw a picture of me as a junior in high school, you would see a pretty, blonde-haired, blue-eyed girl, 5'6" and 118 pounds. That's not what I saw when I looked in the mirror. I thought my thighs curved out where they should curve in. I felt my nose was too big and my lips too small. Standing sideways in the mirror I couldn't tell if my feet were too big or my legs too short, something I first noticed at age ten, but by seventeen, I was *sure* something wasn't right. By this point in my life I determined I was not enough—not smart enough, pretty enough, popular enough, or thin enough. All this external focus covered up the deep internal insecurities I had no idea how to address.

> Our society places an enormous emphasis on appearance. False images of perfection are reinforced everywhere—on television, in film, in print. We measure ourselves and our lives against these unrealistic ideals. Some of us take this to extremes and into the murky world of unattainable perfection. Growing up inside a culture that celebrates a cookie-cutter approach to thinness and beauty, it is easy to see why many young girls develop eating disorders.

We all have different ways to compensate for what we believe we lack. For example, a dominant co-worker might be compensating for a lack of childhood friends or perhaps having been teased in school. A person who excels in the financial world may be reacting to a background of poverty. Others may choose to remain in unfulfilling relationships because they feel unlovable, stemming from a heartbreaking experience in their youth.

I focused on my appearance and weight—something I thought I could control, and a common expression of feeling "not good enough." After relentlessly comparing myself to others who *seemed* to have it together, I concluded, illogically, that I needed to lose weight. My mother was on the "Dolly Parton Diet" and that sounded good to me—fruit the first day, vegetables the next, and fruit and veggies on the third day. The fourth day was the most exciting of all: bananas and milk. I never managed to sustain this diet for long, but it seemed to work anyway. I started to lose weight; and more importantly, people noticed. They noticed and commented. They said, "Have you lost weight?" but I heard, "You look great!" Ah, attention! Just what I had craved.

Later that year I got the flu. I threw up for three days straight. Exhausted and dehydrated, I stepped on the scale after the vomiting subsided, delighted to see how the weight had melted away. I thought, "Look at that! Five pounds magically disappeared!" Something shifted for me.

> Bulimia is an eating disorder characterized by binge eating followed by actions to counteract weight gain such as self-induced vomiting, fasting, or excessive exercise. Due to the shame associated with the disorder, many people do not seek help until after the behavior has become ingrained and is difficult to change.

I began vomiting my food whenever I felt slightly uncomfortable with what I had eaten. I believed I could handle it, but it wasn't long before I realized *it* had *me*. I couldn't stop. I grew increasingly frail and thin. Even I eventually noticed. My concerned friends lovingly fed me my favorite foods to help me grow stronger. This was the attention I had been waiting for.

COLLEGE LIFE

I moved to Boulder, Colorado to attend college. Even with my gaunt frame and strange eating habits I successfully managed to hide my eating disorder from everyone who knew me. There was no need to hide my alcohol and drug use. It seemed everyone liked to party, and there were *many* parties. After the local bars closed for the night we'd either stay up for hours snorting lines of coke, or I would sneak off to binge and vomit. I'd find an excuse to ditch my friends, and I'd drive around aimlessly in the dark, eating.

Of course, I needed a safe place to purge. Often I chose the bathroom at Dunkin Donuts at three in the morning. Or sometimes I found it necessary to throw up in garbage bags in my car. Once I passed out in my car, parked on the side of a mountain road. I woke up to a dreary gray and snowy sky, a garbage bag heavy with vomit sitting on the seat next to me. I felt self-loathing, shame, and disgust. I quietly crept back to my sorority house, promising and swearing I'd never do it again.

The next day, I did it *again*.

My infrequent visits to my eternally supportive therapist kept me alive. She tried everything: anti-depressants from A to Z, hypnosis, a food journal. I couldn't drink with one of the anti-depressants. Needing *some* substance, I turned to smoking pot. I didn't enjoy it as much, but it helped ease my angst.

One afternoon while driving home from one of my rare sanctuaries, the tanning bed, I smoked a joint. When I got out of the car I felt strange. I made it up the stairs to my room when my eyes rolled back into my head, and I collapsed with a seizure. Observing this event, my roommate had had enough—she called my parents.

My parents had had enough as well. An emergency meeting was called with my therapist. They agreed on a plan. I had two weeks to "straighten up" or they threatened to put me into a treatment center immediately. They emphasized either way I was going to treatment— my only choice was *when*. Desperate not to be wrenched from school, I pulled it together, cut back on drugs, and did better with my food, which meant I starved myself to avoid vomiting. I kept a food journal that read something like Monday: apple with peanut butter; bagel and Diet Coke. From my disordered view point, quite a good day. I felt proud—no vomiting, and look at that self-control!

GETTING TREATMENT

As promised, after school ended for the summer, I went to my first treatment center. I learned that "fat" is not actually a feeling. When I *felt* fat, I learned to peer beneath the surface to what might really be going on. This gave me access to expressing some of the deeply buried emotions I usually shoved down with food and then vomited back up. I learned about assertiveness and how to say, "When you said my designer jeans were tacky, that hurt my feelings." (I still wasn't brave enough actually to say this to anyone, but at least I now knew how.)

During my thirty day stay, I absorbed as much as I could and followed the suggestions. I returned to college with hope for my future. For a while I used my new tools and felt strong. But before long, in the same environment filled with partying and all my old patterns, I fell back into my familiar muck.

Now my behavior felt intolerable because I knew something better was possible. At this point, keeping my bulimic behavior a secret was challenging. My shame was unbearable now that my roommate knew why I hid for so long in the bathroom.

During my final months of college, I grew desperate. I hated myself and my life. I felt the buzz of excitement among my friends and classmates as they prepared to begin their new careers, but I was terrified. "What now?" I thought. "I can't do anything!" One particularly gloomy day while wandering aimlessly through the mall during a binge, I glanced at the vacant wall of a yet-to-be-built shop. I imagined a vision of the "hole in my sense of self" that Mark Epstein described. For a moment, staring into the vacant blackness, I clearly saw what I was trying to avoid for all those years. I experienced my fear of graduation approaching; without any clear purpose or direction, I would be lost in this black hole forever. As a child I had eagerly waited for the day I would be launched into adulthood, but now all I could feel was dread. All my life I had avoided pain as best I could. I had repeated patterns that didn't serve me. Now I knew I had actually caused myself more pain by doing so. In that moment at the mall, I was ready for a solution, and I was willing to change.

Aware of my despair, my parents stepped in for the second time. My mom, now sober since 1987, proposed a twelve-step-based treatment center. This time I knew I was ready—I had waited long enough. The night before treatment seemed the longest of my life. My anxiety was intense, but my willingness to change carried me through. Then on my second day in treatment, when the counselor told me I was not only to give up my bulimic practices but alcohol and drugs as well, I was afraid. I called my father and begged him to come get me. "I think you should stay," he said firmly.

That was September 25, 1989, and I chose to stay. My life changed forever on that day. When I made that choice, I began the journey back to myself.

WHAT ARE YOU WAITING FOR?

1. What are some decisions you have made about life, yourself, or others? How have these decisions formed who you have become?
2. What is your relationship with your body—do you love it, hate it, or are your feelings somewhere in between? How does this relationship prevent you from moving forward in your life and from doing what you want?
3. In what ways do you compare yourself?
4. What have you hidden from others about yourself or your life?
5. What methods or behaviors do you use to compensate for any sense of lack?

Practice

> **Personal Responsibility:**
> Societal pressures do exist, but who makes up the society? We do. Who keeps buying the fashion magazines, watching the TV shows? We do. Who keeps falling for the myth that there is something wrong with us? We do. Peer pressure and negative influences exist, but who needs to be responsible for this? We do.

3
Hi Jack

You don't have to see the whole staircase, just take the first step.
Martin Luther King, Jr.

W hen I emerged from the fog of my first few days of treatment, Jack stood there, his twinkling brown eyes smiling at me through thick glasses. He was my counselor for my twenty-eight-day visit.

I met with Jack Schmidt daily to unravel my addictive life and to create something new. On his office wall hung many inspirational sayings including The Desiderata, which is Latin for "desired things." The Desiderata's simple but profound words became the framework for my new life beginning with the instructions: *Go placidly amid the noise and the haste, and remember what peace there may be in silence.* When I left treatment, Jack generously gave me my own copy, which hangs on my wall to this day.

For many of us there is a distinct turning point in life when we stop and assess where we are and where we have been. These are the "ah-ha" moments—something happens and we shift our awareness. These moments take different forms for each of us. It could be the loss of a loved one, an illness, the birth of a child, changing jobs, finishing school, divorce, or as for me, coming to terms with addiction. For some people it can be as simple as awakening one morning and seeing the sunlight reflecting differently on the windowsill. Life is full of these moments where we have an opportunity to choose something new, to re-assess, and to open ourselves to life and its lessons.

For me, in treatment for the second time, I was ready to stop waiting for recovery. I was willing to go to any length to change my behavior. I was eager for instructions on how to live. I had been given the gift of desperation, and it allowed me to open myself to a new way of life. Fortunately this treatment center addressed the whole picture, including my eating disorder, alcohol, and drug use. At the time I had no idea my path to recovery would lead to my life's work.

During treatment we ate breakfast in silence, learning to quiet our minds and be with the food. Frequently counselors led us in guided meditation or read to us. On one occasion, a counselor read *The Precious Present* by Spencer Johnson, MD, which illustrates the gift of living life in the present moment—a concept brand-new to me. This "precious present," the only moment that exists, is an opportunity to let go of all that has happened and all that *might* happen in order just to *be* in the now. Remember all that early waiting and trying to fit in? I had *never* lived in the present. Struck by this simple, yet freeing concept, I vowed always to remember. This was the answer! I would live my life in the present. I would forever have peace. Of course, continuously *remaining* in the present moment is impossible (as I demonstrated repeatedly in my life, most profoundly, when I was waiting for Jack.)

Even while in treatment, staying in the present was challenging. Some days dragged by slowly, thick as mud, while others flew by, and I hardly knew where they went. On one level, I couldn't wait for rehab to end so I could begin my new life, and on another, I wanted to hide in this safe cocoon eternally and never have to face the "real" world. I alternated between excitement and terror about what was to come.

STEPPING INTO THE UNKNOWN

A component of my aftercare plan was to attend recovery meetings for people with addictions. Fresh from treatment, I eagerly attended my first meeting. The room had a smoke-filled haze. At twenty-three, I was the youngest person present. Suddenly, I wasn't sure I was in the right place. I hadn't consumed the quantity of alcohol the others had. I'd never lost a job or had someone leave me because of my addictions. My circumstances *seemed* quite different.

I was concerned, once again, I wouldn't "fit in," but then a fifty-year-old, nearly homeless man spoke words that came straight from my own heart. He expressed thoughts and fears about not belonging, needing alcohol and drugs to fit in, and the emptiness he felt inside. At that moment, I learned to focus on the similarities I shared with these people rather than the differences. I learned the practice of listening without judgment. Really, it was a practice of listening to people share, then judging and assessing everything they said. Was I better off or worse? Did I like them or not? Did I relate to what they shared or feel even more alone? Then I would catch myself judging, let go of my judgment and try not to judge myself for being judgmental! Over and over I practiced letting go of my "terminal uniqueness" that only kept me separate and disconnected. I practiced staying willing and receptive to this novel attitude and new way of life.

As was recommended, I attended ninety meetings in ninety days and opened up more and more to the content and people. These meetings offered a sense of home—we shared similar feelings and life experiences. Each time I left feeling peaceful. I kept going back as I said I would.

> *Kindred spirit—the very fabric of you is so familiar.*
> *It seems as if we are woven of the same thread.*
> Lewis Carter

I established incredible friendships in this new group of supportive people with whom I could share anything (and I reconnected on a deeper level with the dear friends I already had). I created the deep connections I had been waiting and searching for. After hiding shameful secrets for so long, I finally told the truth. I learned to relax and be myself. My new friends and I loved each other through the ups and downs (of which there were many) in our early days of recovery. We explored our spiritual lives together. I read any book on spirituality they recommended and found others on my own. We became the best of friends—more like family. We laughed and cried together. I no longer felt alone.

My friendships continue to be one of my greatest sources of strength. My friends remind me of who I am, even when I forget. They provide unconditional love, support, and encouragement; and I do the same for them.

Practice

> **Develop a Support System**:
> Cultivate deep and meaningful relationships. Find people with whom you can share yourself completely—your dreams, your fears, your secrets—*all of it.* These people can help you stay in the moment, remind you that you are fine as you are—that you don't have to wait for the perfect job, body, or lover to have the life you want.

THIS TOO SHALL PASS

Since I wasn't binging on food or abusing alcohol and drugs, all the emotions I had stuffed away or hidden erupted. Initially, I felt overwhelmed and fragile. I had no idea what to do with these unwelcome thoughts and feelings. A friend suggested I view my mind as a big pot of stew on the stove, with random thoughts and feelings just bubbling to the surface.

"But what do they mean?" I kept asking.

"You don't need to know," my wise friend said. "Just observe your experience without attaching meaning, and let it go."

This idea never occurred to me. I had never considered observing my thoughts and feelings, watching them bubble and pop without reacting to them, without even naming them or thinking about their significance. It was profound (and challenging) to consider they need not be addressed, but could simply be allowed to pass.

The seductive comfort of my addiction, like a siren song luring me toward danger, frequently called to me. I learned what foods, places, or situations triggered my addiction, and I stayed away from them. I avoided anything risky, like a bar or a restaurant that didn't serve food I felt comfortable with. I practiced living one day at a time. Some days were more challenging than others and it was necessary to practice living one minute at a time. I practiced thinking my impulse through to the end. For example, I knew the first sip of beer would open Pandora's Box. I would never know where it would lead. But I was clear, at the very least, it would end with profound despair and resignation. When I thought through this possible scenario, I realized I had gained the power of choice. I could choose it—or not.

I saw how throughout my life, I had been driven by my inability to be with my experience. For example:

> Feeling sad or lonely? The answer was to have a drink.
> Angry? Binge and purge.
> Misunderstood? Isolate and hide from my friends.
> Stressed? Skip class.
> Happy? Celebrate by partying!

Even with all my new-found tools, my feelings continued to dominate my reality. If I didn't *feel* like doing something, I didn't. But I gradually learned to stop making excuses and to follow through on my commitments—even when I didn't feel like it. Just because I didn't feel like getting out of bed and going to work didn't mean I shouldn't go to work! I learned to honor my commitments instead of my thoughts and feelings about my commitments. This gave me a whole new level of freedom, a sense of accomplishment, and personal integrity. This brought me out of waiting, wishing, and wondering and into a place of being in action.

RESPONSIBILITY

In 1990, I met Susan Hansen through my recovery circle. She became the first of many mentors. Susan was big and beautiful in energy and in size and said things like, "I am blown-away-thrilled-to-death-to-be-alive." I adored Susan! Her passion was contagious, and she was a gifted guide to me and many others—a true Goddess! One of the most important lessons she taught was that in any moment we are either in a space of love or a space of fear—and we have a choice about how we live in that space.

I realized the extent to which I allowed fear to tyrannize my life. One old fear that gripped me was of something tragic happening to those I loved. I was terrified of losing my parents, fearing if they were gone, I would really be alone, and I would float off into the ether. Repeatedly Susan told me, "Stop scaring yourself, honey." I started to see *I* was the one scaring myself and I actually did have a choice. I also learned a new definition of responsibility—the ability to respond.

> We can be responsible for our responses to life. Responsibility is a grace we give ourselves. It is not something imposed from outside of us. We have a say in how our life goes.

"No one can make you feel inferior without your consent," Eleanor Roosevelt observed. I discovered that whenever I believed someone else *made* me feel sad, or angry, or even happy, I gave away my power. I learned how to "pause when agitated or doubtful," as it said in the twelve-step literature. First I began to notice when I attributed my feelings to someone or something outside myself. Then, I learned to pause and choose my response.

Over time, I understood that just because I felt something, it didn't make it true. I also realized that my suffering all those years from not feeling good enough had to do with giving away my power. Even if I felt someone (or something) was causing me distress, I didn't have to give power to that feeling. I found that when I didn't respond (or react) to the feeling, I didn't disintegrate. I didn't die from the feeling. That actually, it eventually passed.

I learned that suffering is the difference between how life actually is and how we think it should be. Instead of resisting the ways things are, I could find something to be grateful for. There were no "bad days." A day was simply how it was, and everything else was my interpretation. What seemed to be wrong was merely a product of my thinking, and I whether I liked it or not, I was truly responsible for my happiness or my discontent.

Did I do this perfectly? Far from it! With all this potential expansion, I learned the priceless gift of granting space for my humanity and others' as well. One of the most important lessons I received was the ability to laugh at myself. Frequently the rooms of recovery meetings are overflowing with laughter. Someone unfamiliar with this levity might be shocked by our shared ability to laugh at the absurdity and often the tragedy of our behavior. Laughing at my own humanity provided access to a deeper connection with all of life. I didn't have to be so afraid anymore. I could play in the stream of life. I could embrace my failures.

THE KEYS TO THE KINGDOM

My childhood idea of God was the grandfather image: a man with a long white beard, sitting on his throne in the sky, kindly watching over us. However comforting, my dilemma was that He was *up* there and I was *down* here. God was a great outside force to seek, yet never find. Through my recovery program, I developed my own concept of a "higher power," a God that was also a presence inside all of us.

Those who have hung out in recovery long enough share the common joy of seeing people wake up. So many come defeated and hopeless, but if they stay and do the work, one day the light comes on. To see that spark in someone's eyes is to know something bigger than us exists. This is one of the gifts of service—being there for another's transformation of mind, body and spirit. In working with newcomers, I received the gift of getting out of myself and being of service to another. Instead of sinking into my own morass, I could reach out to someone else and pass along the wisdom that had so freely been given to me. Taking the focus off of me and my problems, I found, was the key to the kingdom.

Gradually over the years, space opened in my brain, cobwebs started to clear, and my mind grew increasingly quiet. I was creating the freedom I needed to stop waiting for my life to begin. I was letting go of the anxiety and the fear of my self-consciousness. I was accepting myself.

My Calling

An unexamined life is not worth living.
Socrates

Ultimately, by following my path of recovery, I profoundly altered my view of life and found my calling. I wanted to be like Susan—an inspiring, loving, powerful mentor who believed in people's greatness— even when *we* forgot. Week after week I would attend Susan's group. Day after day I would attend my meetings. I was retraining myself to live life powerfully, with joy as well as the ability to be with the full range of my experience.

I returned to school and earned a master's degree in mental health counseling. Because of everything I had gone through, I immediately related to the coursework. My understanding deepened, and my knowledge of the mental health field grew.

Existentialist ideas resonated with me—particularly the belief that doubts and fear are part of the human condition. Since there are no guarantees aside from death, angst is natural. This helped to normalize what I had felt for years. I learned fear could provide an opportunity for growth and need not be something to avoid.

I was fascinated, and I thrived. I attained the textbook knowledge to back up all my personal experience. The theories that resonated taught that our lives are a result of the decisions we make at particular turning points. We can allow these decisions to dictate our feelings and behavior, or we can transform our perception. I saw all those early decisions I made about life and myself were not accurate.

> Did my parents' divorce mean anything about me? *Not at all.*

> Am I a failure because I gave a boy a purple fairy doll for a present? *No!*

> What happens if someone thinks my clothes are tacky? *Nothing. It doesn't mean anything about me.*

It all started to make sense and come together. *I* started to make sense.

Through the years, I embraced the twelve-step perspective, and I continued my studies in the field of personal development. I attended many transformational programs, read hundreds of self-help books, and worked with fabulous mentors and coaches. I expanded my spiritual life and experienced a deeper level of peace than ever before. However, my drive to self-destruct wormed its way into my quest for personal development, hidden in the cloak of perfectionism. I selectively ignored the concept of "progress, not perfection." I deceived myself to believe that with enough study and practice, I *would* be "fixed." I would arrive. I would attain perfection. I would find meaning—*the* meaning of life. And *then* I could relax.

But the more I searched for the "answer," the more I missed the point.

And so, on that pivotal day when I recognized I was waiting for Jack, I delved into an inquiry on waiting. I explored the ways I misused self-help. I reflected on my life and everything I had learned—all the lessons, the gifts, the struggles, and the growth. I acknowledged how far I had come since that day in 1989 when I said "yes" to a life of recovery. And I examined all the areas where I *still* waited. I admitted that waiting and looking outside myself for the answers was a pervasive theme in my life. I renewed my commitment to disrupt my *own* ordinary and the ordinary in the world. I interviewed clients and friends, reviewed journals and notes, and researched and reminisced. I collected essays from people who were disrupting the ordinary, and explored what it meant to live an extraordinary life.

What follows is what I found …

WHAT ARE YOU WAITING FOR?

1. Where in your life are you seeking perfection?
2. What are you selectively ignoring in your life?
3. Where are you looking outside yourself for answers?

PART TWO:

MIND

That which we do not bring to consciousness, appears in our lives as fate.
Carl G. Jung

4

JACK OF ALL TRADES, MASTER OF NONE

The true profession of man is to find his way to himself.
Hermann Hesse

M any people spend their lives searching for purpose, waiting to find *the right* thing. Others don't allow themselves to dream. They choose careers based on family expectations and actual (or perceived) pressures from parents and teachers. Some work in jobs they dislike, abandoning the notion they could be happy in their career. They compartmentalize their working lives by saying things such as, "It's just a job—I don't need to like it. I can enjoy my time off and wait for retirement."

In the past, I frequently asked myself, "What am I going to be when I grow up?" Inevitably, the next question was, "When, exactly, will I grow up?"

Being a grownup never seemed like a good idea to me. I felt unsure of myself for so long; why would I want the responsibility that comes with being an adult? On the other hand, I entertained the illusion that growing up was somehow a point of arrival—when you got *there,* no more mysteries. Everything would be clear, certain. But then I wondered, "How would I know I *had* arrived? When would I be sure?"

WAITING FOR PURPOSE

I urgently searched for the "right thing," some external force that would take me down the right path. I waited to *feel* inspired. I looked for purpose as if it were a buried treasure I would surely find if only I could locate the map.

As a child, I don't remember ever having a deep passion to be *one* specific thing—other than a horse, galloping around with the wind rushing through my tangled mane. I was a daydreamer, so it was not surprising my report cards mostly read "effort inconsistent," "unsatisfactory," and "having difficulty." I never liked to study. I never believed I was good at it.

While grappling with addiction in college, I floundered through my courses. Art history was the only subject that didn't feel too threatening or overwhelming. I had grown up in an artsy family: Dad was an art historian and curator, and Mom was a talented artist. I really liked looking at art and discovering the deeper meaning. I wondered what the artists were thinking as they created. What emotions lay behind their forms, colors, and shapes? What were they trying to say?

I enjoyed this form of inquiry, so I decided to take a psychology class. Unfortunately, my sporadic attendance led to an event one hopes would be relegated to the realm of nightmares and never surface in real life. One day, I arrived at class as the professor handed out the midterm exam! Terror twisted my stomach into knots. I desperately wanted to run, but I sat there in a cold sweat and hoped my unpreparedness wasn't too obvious to my classmates. I skimmed the test, searching for something, *anything* I could answer. Not surprisingly, I failed.

Ironically, it was after college in treatment that I discovered my passion for the field of psychology and personal growth. I immersed myself, volunteering at a domestic violence crisis center while I earned a master's degree. Later, I worked in treatment centers similar to the one that had helped me recover. For eight years, I had focus and a tremendous desire to assist others on their journey. Then in 1998, shortly after moving back to Colorado, the treatment center where I worked went out of business and I was laid off.

I sat at a crossroads. I loved my work, but when I interviewed for other jobs in the field, I realized I was burned out. The sadness I had witnessed among the clients I came to know and care about overwhelmed me. I knew recovery and wellness were possible. Yet time and time again, I watched patients return to their addictions which often led to the collapse of their lives.

The answer, it seemed, was to try something new. I believed the solution was to go to school, school, and more school. During the years that followed, I pursued massage therapy, real estate, and even had a brief stint as a boutique owner. Each time, I enjoyed my work for awhile then gradually grew dissatisfied and looked for the next right thing. Each time I hoped "maybe *this* will be it!" Maybe I would again find my sense of purpose.

Is our purpose locked away inside? Or do we get to create it? Do we go along through life and hope that one day it knocks on the door? "Hello, it's me, your purpose. You have been looking for me all this time and here I am!" Many of us have been waiting for just that. I know I was.

You will find your vocation where the world's needs and your talents meet.
Aristotle

Even as I wandered, I continued my studies and exploration in the field of personal development. I attended training courses and workshops. I listened to lectures. I assisted others on their path of self-discovery but still I didn't know what I wanted to do. Then one day a dear friend recommended Jack Canfield's book, *The Success Principles*. I read it eagerly, and for the first time, I did an extensive exercise on creating a vision for my life.

Through this profound exercise, I saw all roads lead to *this* place. I realized all my careers and life experiences helped form who I became, but I am so much more than my job. I saw that while there was nothing wrong being a "Jack of all trades," it was (once again) my old familiar tendency to search outside myself for the answers and to wait for my life really, finally to begin.

I recalled an art history professor sharing the story of Michelangelo. After sculpting the *David*, he was asked how he created such a magnificent work of art. Michelangelo responded he simply removed all the stone that *wasn't* the *David*. Maybe my purpose *was* buried under the surface and I could remove what stood in my way—my doubts, fears and limitations. Or maybe I could create it daily. Perhaps it would change as I went through life. Possibly I would always wonder. But now it was no longer a matter of searching for purpose. I realized I could construct it. I could *create* it. I could choose what and who I was going to be. Soon I began to inquire and contemplate what might be possible in the world if *everyone* realized this for themselves. I re-created myself as a coach, which is really *who* I have been all along.

Practice

> **Cultivating Satisfaction:**
> There is nothing wrong with wanting to find a career that is a true expression of who you are, but first inquire—are you happy with yourself? Start there, do the work that it takes to be content, and you can be satisfied in any job. From that place you can create and find a new career—*or not.*

CREATION

We need not follow an elusive and mystical journey to that special day when we find our true purpose. Our purpose is available for all of us right now. By exploring our natural aptitudes, talents, preferences, and attractions, we can define (and design) our purpose. We don't have to wait until we are *sure.* We have endless choices and options. And, we can always change our minds.

I never considered myself to be gifted with creativity. I compared my rudimentary artwork to my mother's extreme talent. I measured my inadequate knowledge of art history against my father's lengthy career as an art historian and consultant. It was easy to conclude that I lacked the innate ability. It wasn't until recently that I have let myself express my own creativity, to define what that means for me. Creativity *may* come easier for some than others. But just because it seems more difficult doesn't mean the creativity doesn't exist. Individual expressions of creativity differ from person to person.

Being an adult can be a highly creative act when we:

> Focus on the journey, not the destination—and allow ourselves to explore other routes.
>
> Let ourselves enjoy life and have fun.
>
> Allow ourselves to live fully and continue to grow.
>
> Remain curious and open to the adventure.

SUCCESS

I realized by keeping myself sick all those years, I never let myself shine or excel. I was both afraid to fail *and* afraid to succeed. I was afraid I might threaten people if I did shine, so I hid in the herd. I self-sabotaged, and I played it safe by never allowing myself to dream.

As a society, we have external measures that define success: social and economic status, the school we attend, or our title at work. We think of success as an arrival point, a destination we wait to reach. And once we get there, we hope we can stay. However this arrival point is often an arbitrary set of measurements based on other people's ideas of success. Problems occur when we measure who we are by what we have or have not done.

I didn't set goals because I *knew* I would fail. I had broken so many promises to myself over the years. I would fail an exam and promise myself I would study next time. I would binge and purge and promise to stop. During my addiction, I was incapable of keeping my promises. I had to learn I could trust myself to do what I said I would do.

Many of us decide we have failed before we even begin. Sometimes we believe it will be easier to admit to ourselves that we didn't succeed because we didn't really try. We don't like to think we tried our best but couldn't succeed. Not trying keeps us safe; it protects our fragile egos.

When we don't try, we cheat ourselves. We don't give ourselves the lessons and experiences it takes to succeed. Failure is just a part of the journey and is a necessary component of success. "Success," said Winston Churchill, "is the ability to go from failure to failure with no loss of enthusiasm."

One of humanity's greatest strengths is resiliency—the ability to adapt to varied conditions, overcome setbacks, and continue to grow. Each of us has this ability, and it is our resilience that gives us strength. To play it safe is to miss the opportunity to make the necessary mistakes that form the foundation for great success—*whatever success means to you.*

Let's define success for ourselves. What might be possible then? What if we measured our success by the joy we experienced and what we shared with others on our journey?

And the real issue is not whether or not we are going to fail, but rather who we are going to *be* when we do.

Practice

> **Commitment:**
> Commit to something that is important to you and take action, no matter what. As we have all heard before, feel the fear and do it anyway. Don't wait for the *right* moment. Apply for that new job or take that class you've always wanted to. Take the first steps *today.* Surround yourself with people who support you in

achieving your dreams and goals and who listen to and for your greatness.

Build New Habits:
Create new habits that support your growth. Begin by changing one self-sabotaging habit to a self-enhancing one. For example, start the day well by meditating or journaling instead of turning on the TV. Create a structure for yourself which aligns with your goals. Have a plan and honor it throughout the day.

REMEMBER, IT IS NEVER TOO LATE

For her fortieth birthday, my mother received flying lessons as a gift. By age fifty-one she was a Flight Engineer on a Boeing 727 jet. She became an airline captain at age fifty-six. Any time I say to myself, "Oh, I can't do that ..." all I have to do is think of my mother. Her passion for flying surpassed all evidence that "proved" her dream impossible.

Everything you have ever done has led you to where you are now; everything that lies ahead is an opportunity. None of it is wasted. It's all part of who you are and what you can become. Experience, pleasant or otherwise, provides the ingredients that hone skills, form abilities, and make you special. It's your unique offering to the world.

As you continue to evolve and practice mastery of whatever interests you, it is the experience of this growth and practice that provides fulfillment.

When I lose sight of my vision or my fear of failure (or of success) creeps in, I meditate on George Bernard Shaw's brilliant words: "I rejoice in life for its own sake. Life is no 'brief candle' for me. It is a sort of splendid torch which I have got hold of for the moment, and I want to make it burn as brightly as possible before handing it on to future generations."

WHAT ARE YOU WAITING FOR?

1. What are your dreams?
2. What attempts have you made to make these dreams reality?
3. What messages did you get about success growing up? Are you letting that stop you?
4. What does success mean to you today?
5. Are you willing to let yourself fail?
6. Are you waiting for your purpose to knock on your door, or are you actively creating it?

ESSAYS ON DISRUPTING THE ORDINARY

"Waiting for Life" by Jessica Lewis

My husband's job led us overseas, and by rules of the contract, I cannot obtain employment easily in my new country. When I found out we were coming here, I was excited about the experience I'd have of living overseas. My chance had come to do and search for the thing I've wanted in my life but couldn't define. My chance to discover the thing I've been waiting to discover.

Sometimes I remind myself of what I haven't yet done in life. I think about how I completely missed out on backpacking through Europe. I wanted to. I was poor in college, but mostly I missed out because I was afraid to make it happen.

But now, I am in Korea. One thing I decided before I got here was that I wouldn't make that mistake of being afraid again. I've toured all over Korea, sampled the food, learned the customs and the language. I still have plans for more.

For *two years* I'll live here. I need to do something else with my ample free time. Not make lists about what to do when I return to Colorado, when I can have a job again, but *now*. I don't want to look back in ten years and say, "While I was in Korea I should have ..." Fill in the blank.

Hadn't I made *this* a reality? Am I not a composer of my life? I'm, at the least, an editor. Right? Yes. I put it out there in my heart of hearts that I wanted an experience far away from Colorado, far away from my tiny orchard-farming hometown in upstate New York. And here I am in Korea. I had a hand in that.

Writing is a passion and a joy I've always kept hidden from others. But here in my new country I'm a blank slate. I have time to work at it.

It occurs to me, almost by surprise, that I have added a plot twist to my own life. I have a fairly large group of friends who are published, or have forthcoming books or articles. There are seven at least. How odd it seems that I've collected these friends, these writers, who don't even know—have no idea—that this is a passion of mine. Have I willed this unknowing support group for myself too?

Yes.

You see, I do know. I did *already* know what I wanted to do, what I am ... *was* waiting to do. I just had to turn the pages of my own life, reread the good chapters, the best parts, like a favorite book. I've stopped waiting for my life to begin.

5
JACK OF HEARTS

Plant your own garden and decorate your own soul instead
of waiting for someone to bring you flowers.
From the poem "After a While" by Veronica A. Shoffstall

Until I got into recovery, I was convinced there wasn't enough love to go around, and I found "proof" everywhere. No matter how many men I dated, no matter how many love letters I received, the Jack of Hearts kept eluding me. I couldn't get enough love—or the right kind of love—to *make* me feel complete.

As a teenager, I pasted the poem "After a While" on the wall of my room. Over and over I read the suggestion to stop waiting for someone to bring me flowers. But wait I did. I indulged in the fantasy of wanting a man to save me, fix me, and rescue me. I waited for my Prince Charming, *the one* who could ride in, sweep me off my feet, and carry me off to a beautiful, love-filled, Technicolor life—and save me from myself.

In addition to looking for the wrong thing, I searched in the wrong places. I thought if I slept with a man, he would fall in love with me. While that occasionally led to a relationship, it usually left me feeling empty and ashamed.

On the other extreme, I dated a lot of jealous men. "If only my boyfriend (whichever one it happened to be at the time) didn't need so much reassurance," I reasoned, "the relationship might work." Secretly, I felt their jealousy validated me. It showed I was important and loved—and *worthy* of the jealousy. Although I complained about their jealousy and neediness, all along I hid my own.

If there was any sign the relationship was ending, I was out the door. I knew what it was like to *feel* abandoned. I carried out my earlier vow never to be left again.

Yet I wondered why most of my relationships didn't work out ...

We say we want love, but instead of cultivating it internally, we wait for Prince (or Princess) Charming to arrive and make all the hurt and pain go away.

> If we don't take the time to identify our relationship patterns and underlying belief systems, we never get the chance to understand why we adopted them and allow ourselves to see how they are impacting our lives. If we don't examine this, we may prevent ourselves from ever finding true satisfaction.

I ask my clients, "Do you know it's not someone else's job to make you happy?" Most of them immediately answer, "Of course I do!" Then I ask them to take a closer look.

Relationships frequently become another way we look outside ourselves for validation and for answers. We develop patterns that begin in childhood. We take what we know, what is familiar, what we saw growing up, and incorporate this into our lives. We look at our role models and decide to be like them—or vow never to do what *they* did. From this position, often we choose a partner just like our parents—or just the opposite of them.

Most of us say we know we are responsible for our own satisfaction, but deep down we still *wait* for that someone to appear who will make us happy. Hoping they will have the magic key to unlock our heart. We want to believe in fairy tales where all our needs and wishes will be met and we live happily ever after.

We want guarantees and promises. From all the love stories and songs that surround us, we know how love is supposed to go. Yet, how it is *supposed* to go is usually not how it *actually* goes.

To further complicate matters, deep down, we are afraid of being alone. Despite our desire for love, often we don't know how to let love in. Fear of abandonment causes many people to go through life protecting their hearts and never knowing true intimacy. Allowing someone to know us, letting them draw close, exposes us to the possibility of being hurt, so many times we don't share who we really are—we protect our soft underbellies and put on our hard, outer shells.

We also see relationships as the end result. We tell ourselves, "When I get *there*, everything will be okay. When I have my first boyfriend, first kiss, first love, get married, have a child (or two) … then I will have everything I want." We get the relationship, the newness wears off, the luster fades, and we often blame our partner for failing to meet our expectations.

EXPECTATIONS: PREMEDITATED RESENTMENTS

Expectations are our rules and guidelines for how relationships should go, how our partners should behave, and what love should look like.

Examples of these unspoken rules are:

> If they really loved me they wouldn't _____.

> They should know better! They know I don't like it when they_____.

> They know I like _____! Why didn't they do that (or get that) for me?

We make up these rules (often forgetting we made them up) and then fail to inform our partner—we expect them to know because, after all, they *said* they loved us! We believe they should follow our rules, and we become resentful when they don't. Our expectations are usually proportionate to the depth of our relationships—the closer we are to someone, the higher our expectations.

GUILTY BEFORE PROVEN INNOCENT

My friend Peter was complaining to me about his wife. She had been away all week on business, and he really missed her. When she got home, she took a call from her business partner and was on the phone for an hour. He started building a case. "This should be *my* time, and she should want to spend it with me. She was with her partner all week. Why didn't she miss me like I missed her?"

He was incensed *and* convinced his wife was guilty of not loving him enough. Midway through his rant, he realized all his wife did was talk on the phone. It didn't have anything to do with him! He saw his feelings of hurt were a pattern stemming from his childhood when he didn't get the attention he wanted. This realization allowed him to gain perspective, calm his fears, and view the situation rationally. He was able to let go of his expectations and simply love her.

One of my dysfunctional patterns is to interpret someone's tone of voice. The pattern looks like this: First, I decide there is actually a tone without considering that the tone—if it even exists—may have nothing to do with me. Then I tell myself what the tone means—and usually it is not a positive interpretation. Since I am highly trained, a former therapist after all, I decide I am right! Then I react to what I have made up and sometimes cause an argument. Only later do I realize that the other person never meant anything by his or her tone. I can even do this with strangers! Or even more ludicrous, I interpret the tone of emails. This is a good time to bring in the valuable tool of laughing at myself and employ my ability to make amends for my behavior.

WELCOME THE MULTITUDE OF OPPORTUNTIES TO LEARN

Misunderstanding and disagreement in any relationship can actually be an opportunity to learn about ourselves. However, most of the time we simply focus on how the other person is *wrong*. It is easier to point the finger than to look to ourselves and face the unpleasant truth that we may share some or all of the responsibility. We think, "If he (or she) were only more considerate, had more time for me, or did the dishes more, *then* I'd be happy."

Instead of looking at our own behavior, we believe that the other person is the problem. We believe we are justified, reasonable and more than fair. *They* need to change.

Of course, it is human nature to want to be right. Most arguments start with small issues and escalate. Problems grow the longer we hold our positions. We gather evidence, adding fuel to the fire, and over time, we lose sight of the original issue. What we are left with is, at best, distance in a relationship, and at worst, no relationship at all.

Examples of this kind of interaction are everywhere. Longstanding feuds between families going back generations may have begun with something as simple as a careless comment or a misinterpreted glance. Or the reason could be something equally insignificant as leaving dirty socks on the floor.

When I believe I am right, I spend an exorbitant amount of time re-hashing the situation in my mind. I obsessively review the other person's responses and actions to find the evidence I need to be right. In this internal dialogue, nothing changes. I try to build my case, yet I get nowhere. If I continue down this path, when the time comes to discuss the matter with the other person, I've already become the judge, jury, and executioner.

Recently, in an interaction with one of my best friends, I felt hurt by something she did. Now this should *always* be my first indication to realize I am self-righteously attached to my point of view. Instead, I started gathering evidence to support my position. The obvious conclusion: she didn't love me enough. "Enough for what?" might be the question on your mind. And that is precisely the dilemma. In this less-than-enlightened state, *there is no "enough."*

The movie *Jerry Maguire* is one of my favorites. Yet the line, "you complete me," that the main character wooingly says to his love interest, is a slippery slope. We are complete already. Isn't it time we know this?

Although my irrational thoughts told me one thing (that she didn't love me enough), my healed self became willing to be responsible and acknowledged that I was blaming her for my feelings. I apologized to her for my behavior. Miraculously, something new emerged. A new space of authenticity opened up between us. I realized (again) the gift of being responsible for myself, and I saw that I could return to my commitment to love without attachment and without strings.

It really does take more energy to hold on to being right than it does simply to be responsible for our behavior. When we are willing to let go, problems can be solved more easily. People are more willing to listen, to be open, and even to acknowledge responsibility when they are not under attack.

Practice

Identify Your Expectations:
First acknowledge you have expectations. Then ask yourself if you are willing to give them up. Stop expecting others to read your mind, to know what you want and need, and to satisfy your unspoken expectations. Stop *waiting* for people to *complete* you.

Stop Keeping Score:
Yesterday's argument doesn't have to carry over. Don't bring it into your next dispute. Don't throw things in each other's faces. Accept

that we are all human. We all make mistakes. We have our moods, our reactions, our fears.

Acceptance:
Love people for who they *are* and who they *aren't.* Allow them to change and grow. Be willing to see them newly. Don't put them in a box. Instead of trying to make them be who you want them to be, give them the space to be who they are.

Give Up Being Right:
Ask yourself—how important is your position, really? Is being right more important than your relationships?

BE THE ONE TO FORGIVE

Forgiveness could be defined as "to give as before." Before we formed all our expectations, opinions, and judgments. Before we were hurt or afraid of being hurt. Before we closed off parts of our heart. Before we were sure we were right.

We all are capable of a great deal more than we realize. Pope John Paul II forgave his would-be assassin, and Nelson Mandela forgave the prison guards who abused him. These examples represent an almost inconceivable level of forgiveness. Yet *we* hold on to the small grudges. "I don't like how my husband snapped at me this morning. He shouldn't talk to me like that." Or "I don't like that tone my co-worker used." Imagine what would be possible if we were willing to stop holding grudges, to stop being petty. To stop waiting until we're "ready" to forgive.

Why forgive? Because forgiveness is a gift we give to others and to ourselves. It breaks the chains of anger, fear, and hate that bind us. It lets the past be what it is—the past. It allows us, and those we forgive, to move on. It opens up something new for today and tomorrow.

Or we can forgive simply for the sake of forgiveness.

Practice

Don't Wait:
Be willing to be the first to let go. The first to say "I am sorry". The first to say "I love you." Do it out of a sense of honor and not from a place of martyrdom or victimization. If your motivation is to be superior or "I guess I have to be the one *again,*" you are missing the point.

When You Forgive, Be Generous:
Don't forgive partially or hold back. Forgive fully. Be gracious in your forgiveness. Let the other person off the hook. Be willing to take the high road, to be responsible. Remember you will benefit greatly.

COME FROM LOVE

Real love has no expectations, no rules, and no demands. When we judge people, we disconnect from them. Our constant judging keeps us locked up inside, separated from what we really want, which is to be connected. We are either in a state of love or a state of fear—we can't experience both at the same time. When we judge, we do not love. When we judge *how* someone loves us, we are not being loving.

When we practice self-observation, we notice how often we feel the need to be right and to judge others. With perspective, we gradually let go of needing to be right. We come to understand that making someone else wrong is not a loving act. We value our differences as well as our similarities. We embrace our humanity as we learn to cherish the humanity of others.

When we learn to look through the lens of love, we shift our point of view. We find ways to turn negative situations into positive ones.

Practice

> **Open Your Heart to Love:**
> Love the thunderstorm that delayed and drenched you on your way to your job interview. Love the drivers who let you cut in front of them (or who cut you off). Love everything from the sweet taste of chocolate to a gentle backrub.

To love oneself is the beginning of a lifelong romance.
Oscar Wilde

The most important thing we can do is to learn to love and accept ourselves. We can get to know ourselves as well as we can, find our likes and dislikes, and spend time alone and learn to enjoy our own company. If we don't enjoy our own company, no one else will.

From the space of self-love, we can enter into a relationship and *be* the person with whom we would want a relationship.

The truth is that we can have love even when we are not in a romantic relationship. We can love our friends, family, pets, what we do, and where and how we live. If we believe we are not loveable, we will never find the real love or satisfaction we seek. We can find fulfillment for ourselves and stop demanding that others fulfill us.

Practice

> **Get on the Court:**
> It is difficult to learn how to be in a relationship when you are not in one. You wouldn't try to learn how to play tennis by sitting on your couch watching Wimbledon. You might pick up some good pointers, but you won't actually be playing the game. Consider that relationships don't need to look a particular way. Just get out there on the court and play.

Don't Wait for Love:
Just simply get out there and love. Do you know you can love someone without being loved back? Allow your heart to be broken—love with abandon. Love big, messy love.

Give Up Knowing:
If we assume we know how another is going to relate to us, we leave the other person with no room to be any other way. Embrace the spirit of discovery.

In any relationship, we can practice seeing one another as two equals coming together, two complete beings interacting to form a union. Another's light does not diminish our own. More than one star lights up the heavens. We are actually the source of love in our relationships. We don't have to wait for our "Jack of Hearts" to fulfill us. Love doesn't come from somewhere outside of us. We can generate love any time we choose. Love never runs out. There is enough light for all of us. There is enough love to go around. *And* we can be compassionate with ourselves when we temporarily forget all of this.

My women's group—a group of six of us that have been meeting monthly for the last two years—took on the credo created by my angelic friend Dusty. These instructions really sum up the messages of this chapter:

1. Go out into the world.
2. Create relationships.
3. Love unabashedly.
4. Make mistakes.
5. Access things you "may" want to heal.
6. Forgive your humanity.
7. Thank God for the process and opportunity.
8. Love yourself unabashedly.
9. Repeat Steps 1-8 until the day you die.

IF IT IS TIME TO LEAVE, LEAVE FROM LOVE

How often do we let go of a relationship because we "just fell out of love" or "felt it just wasn't there anymore?"

It's like walking into a home with a nice fire burning in the wood stove. We stand in front of the stove and soak up its warmth because it feels *so* good. Predictably, after a while the fire dies down. If we related to the wood stove the way we approach love, we would stand in front of the stove and demand more warmth. We would tell the stove, "I will give you more wood as soon as you provide more heat." It may sound ridiculous, but that's what we do.

Tend to the fire so that it continues to give warmth. You might need to put new kindling in the stove, and you might need to relight it.

Many relationship dilemmas can be solved by practicing the principles in this chapter. And sometimes it is time to simply move on. If it is truly time to leave a relationship, take the challenge and leave from love. We don't have to destroy one another to justify that it's time to go. We can love another and still choose not to stay together anymore.

PERFECTLY HUMAN

I finally realized that love is both a way of being and an action. I met my husband a year before we started dating. I spotted him across the room. Inexplicably I found myself wanting to be near him. Sure, he was nice to look at, but it was more than that. I've seen (and dated) plenty of attractive men. So what was it about him? It was a "peaceful, easy feeling." It was something I can't quite describe. I wanted to *know* this man. We bumped into each other several times over the next year, and one day he asked for my number. I had no fear or doubt; I just knew he would call. On our second date, he handed me a poem:

> *I saw an Angel today.*
> *I know because she left a golden thread in my car.*

I saw it fall as she stepped out,
As if purposefully placed.
So I would not forget she had come.
Or maybe so I would not think it a dream.
But there is no dream to compare to this.
For me she has landed,
I know I saw the gods smile.

We came together as two equals. We chose each other. We took time to create and design our relationship, to understand and align on our dreams and goals. We developed a deep friendship. We shared a spiritual path and a life of sobriety.

It's not always poems and peace. We have our ups and downs—our minor disagreements and our major difficulties. Sometimes what we want to do is *run*. For a moment, we may even believe it might be better with someone else. Maybe that perfect Prince (or Princess) charming *is* out there somewhere yet to be discovered. Maybe we should keep waiting for the Jack of Hearts. And then we catch ourselves. We remember who we are. And we return to our love and our commitment—our mutual respect and our choice. As the years pass, issues that used to last a few days or even a week now last (at most) a few hours. When the storm passes, we laugh together at what once seemed so significant. We have learned what it takes to disrupt the ordinary in our relationship. We strive to embrace each other's humanity—and laugh at ourselves when we are unwilling to do so.

WHAT ARE YOU WAITING FOR?

Examine your beliefs and feelings about love by answering the following questions:

1. Where are you waiting for love?
2. What does love mean to you?
3. What has it meant in the past?
4. What do you want it to mean?

ESSAYS ON DISRUPTING THE ORDINARY

"This Is It?" *by Jessica Wilson*

We had been together eight years, married for four. "Settled in" to our home, our careers, and our marriage. Predictable, uninteresting, habitual. From the outside, life looked pretty great for us. But for me, there was an emptiness. A question—*"This is it?"* Don't get me wrong, there was nothing in particular that was bad, it just wasn't what I had pictured married life to be. I thought it would be surprise roses, candlelit dinners, and spontaneous sex all the time. I thought it would be prince charming sleeping next to me every night. But there he was, more like a frog, snoring and smelly, every morning. *"This is it?"* This *was* it. I complained about him to my friends, that the arguments were always the same. He hated the way I cooked, and I hated the way he belittled my cooking. He wished I would make more of an effort to be nice to him, and I wondered why he couldn't just be nice to me first. He said if I was happy, he was happy; and I felt the same way. But neither of us was willing to do the work, to be the one to let go of the rope that we were tugging.

The truth was, when we both *really* looked, we loved each other dearly and couldn't see ourselves apart. Our relationship just needed some attention and re-creation.

After doing some soul-searching and research, we decided to attend a personal development seminar. What became clear during that weekend was that I could declare, "I have an extraordinary marriage," and I did! My actions became consistent with that declaration and became the driving commitment to my marriage. And this was just *my* commitment! It had nothing to do with what my husband was doing! I decided that when I spoke of my husband, it would always be complimentary and loving. I wasn't going to be one of those women who constantly complained about their spouse *anymore*. I took up forgiving him, and it became a practice for me. When I saw my tendency to jab and poke at him, I quickly found my love for him and forgave him for his flaws, just to forgive him.

I loved him for all that he was, and all that he wasn't. And that was the key. The man of my dreams was there all along, and I have never been happier. And neither has he! Our marriage is now the kind of marriage I once dreamed of.

6

JACK AND JILL WENT UP THE HILL

No matter where you go, there you are.
Confucius

In 1989 at a recovery meeting, I was stunned when I heard the term "geographical cure," as it summed up so much of my life. It refers to the illusion that life will be better when we get somewhere *else*. So we expectantly wait until we get *there* and "there" is somewhere, anywhere other than where we are right now. We think, "I'll be happy when I climb that hill. When I go on vacation. When I am at the beach. When I live in that kind of house. When I finally visit that country or state." We *wait* to be in the "right" place. We wait for that place magically to change what's wrong in our lives. What we forget is that we take ourselves and all of our baggage with us wherever we go.

Certain places are magical, wondrous, and desirable. Who doesn't think about their own insignificance when viewing the magnificent expansiveness of the Grand Canyon? Religious sages went to majestic mountaintops to commune with God. Throughout history, pioneers explored uncharted territories such as the western United States with hopes, visions, and dreams of creating something better.

Places help us see our place in the world, if we let them. Places can help us grow, and learn. However (as was my tendency), we can look at them as one more thing outside ourselves where the answer lies.

A geographical cure "fixes" problems by changing where we are, moving our location, or shifting things around. This way we can avoid looking inside to the source of our problems and their cause. Sometimes our problems go away temporarily, but inevitably they return.

You can't put a jackass on a plane and expect it to get off as a racehorse. But try we will. This is the false hope of the geographical cure.

ON THE GO

Mark, a salesman, tells the following story: "My father was in the army, so when I was growing up, we moved constantly. Just as I was about to settle in, we would move, and I would once again say goodbye to my friends, teachers, and home. But I didn't even know what home was. I vowed when I was able to decide for myself, I would put down roots and never move again.

"When I got my first job after college, I picked a town and set my sights there. For the first year, it was great. I knew everyone in town. I spent weekends doing yard work or hanging out with the neighborhood guys. Then I started to get uneasy. I found myself being short-tempered and annoyed with my friends. I started reading travel magazines and hung pictures of different places throughout my home. Soon, I put my house on the market and moved across the country. Shortly after moving into my new house and town, I dreamt I was packing to move again.

"The next morning, I had an epiphany: I couldn't be with myself! I was the problem. Not where I lived. I had never gotten used to the quiet of my own company."

Mark, like many of us, tried to escape from his unhappiness by moving. But until he unpacked his own baggage, he couldn't be happy *anywhere* he went. Until he sat still with himself, he was doomed to keep *waiting* for his happiness and his life to begin.

ROCKY MOUNTAIN HIGH

I attempted to escape by leaving the East Coast and heading to the foothills of the Colorado Rockies for college. The allure of the meditative sage on the mountaintop always appealed to me. I fantasized about finding peace and freedom from myself in the mountains. I hoped that by living "up high" I would have the perspective I needed to straighten out my life. Colorado seemed like the right combination of "far enough away" and "different enough from home."

My love affair with climbing hills began in 1982 when my father introduced me to the West. We took a trip to a small guest ranch in Wyoming. Something inside of me expanded as I stood in the middle of nowhere, surrounded by towering peaks and vast acres of national forest.

At the ranch, it was easy to forget there was another world out there. As we exited the pavement, I left many of my concerns behind and began the bumpy ride on the rutted dirt road to paradise. Days were filled with swimming in frigidly cold high mountain lakes and streams and lazy rides on the horses. Of course, my favorite experiences were the long hikes to the tops of various peaks where I could view the world from a different perspective. I found quiet and serenity for a brief moment, and I craved more of that.

For many years, our Wyoming vacations provided a constant for me amid a life of much change—back and forth between households, off to college, my many ups and downs. The ranch served as my anchor, holding passing memories of magical times. No matter how sick I felt, I always found a sense of tranquility during my Wyoming visits.

When it was time to choose a college, I headed west. Although Colorado itself didn't fix me as I had hoped, I still fell in love with it. When I left for treatment, I was heartbroken. I would hear John Denver singing and cry—it reminded me of all I had missed.

> *And the Colorado Rocky Mountain high*
> *I've seen it rainin' fire in the sky*
> *You can talk to God and listen to the casual reply ...*

In recovery, I realized that although I had looked to Colorado as an escape, it also provided me with an experience of life that I loved. It allowed me to connect with myself in profound ways.

THE BENEFITS OF PLACE

As Cindy describes it, "I never understood the appeal of the mountains until I moved to Colorado. During the summer, many of my friends climbed the famous Fourteeners throughout the state (Colorado has fifty-four 14,000-foot peaks). Although I loved the mountains, I always said no to their requests to join them. After a particularly persuasive friend asked for the tenth time, I finally said yes. It was only then that I realized how afraid I was. The group was kind and patient with me, knowing it was my first ascent. We started in the misty early morning, dressed in layers, carrying light packs and plenty of water. As we climbed, the clouds parted, the expansive view opened up, and I was moved beyond belief. In the silence of the morning, I realized why my friends were so eager to take this trek. In the vastness of it all, I saw the insignificance of my fears and concerns. Had I listened to my fears, I never would have had this moment. I then saw my thoughts were what kept me trapped in life—really they were my *only* limitations. I felt connected to this group of travelers, to nature, and to something bigger than all of us. I experienced the glory and power of it all, and at the same time I realized I could carry this knowledge with me wherever I went."

When we stop and smell the roses, many of us can attest that being in nature gives us definite psychological benefits. It restores our mental clarity, provides us with an increased sense of well-being, and can reduce our stress levels. For others, immersion into the bustle of city life is just the ticket.

In a new place, we often gain perspective on our lives. Places assist us in finding ourselves in the microcosm of the macrocosm. They allow us to hear our inner voice amidst all the clamor and noise. Places can teach us to look inside in a new way, to find a sense of connection—not only to the place, but more importantly to ourselves.

Conscious Discovery

No house or hill will save us from our own mind. At some point we have to stop running away and learn to enjoy our own company. Some people will spend eternity moving around to avoid being with themselves. Once again, we have an opportunity to find a balance. We may desire a place where we can put down roots, but we may also wish to seek, visit, and explore.

Often when I travel, I try places on. Sometimes the line between old behavior (the seeking of the geographical cure) and my inquisitiveness is faint. I wonder, "Would I like it better here? What would my life be like? Would I be happier?" I have even gone as far as spending the day with a realtor. Each time I go through this, I see hidden aspects of myself. Sometimes I discover that I am craving change. Sometimes I just don't want to go back to work on Monday. Sometimes I think a *different* set of hills will do the trick. And most importantly, I discover that I don't have to judge my process.

Each of us has the opportunity to examine this for ourselves—are we powerfully choosing, or are we looking for an escape? No matter where we go, we take *us* along. On the other hand, we can create a sense of home anywhere, and some places will always remain special.

Practice:

Being Aware:

Stop and consider the places you have been. What have they taught you? Have you learned to be with yourself? Do you use a move or vacation to run from your problems or yourself? Are you waiting to find the right place? To live in (or visit) the right environment— and then you will be happy? Is this a pattern?

Or have you achieved balance? What does that balance look like for you?

We shape our dwellings, and afterwards our dwellings shape us.
Winston Churchill

The allure of the hills was what brought me back to Colorado. But by then I believed (even when I forgot) that the key to my happiness lies in the inner landscape, not the outer one.

Fortunately, my husband was willing to give up living by the ocean for our shared vision of a little house on the side of a hill. After some years in Colorado, we found our dream home: a magical little house on the side of a mountain at the end of a very long dirt road. The first time we visited the house, we ended up walking the length of the mile-long, Jeep-trail of a road, through a grove of shimmering Aspen, hearing the sound of the leaves rustling in the breeze. It all felt so familiar and powerfully reminded me of the ranch in Wyoming. As we continued to walk closer, a dramatic view mysteriously and magically began to emerge. A vast expanse of mountains, layered over other mountains, and cloud striations. The road ended at the sweet profile of a house perched on the side of the hill, looking out over the magnificent and awe-inspiring view. It was quiet. Utterly peaceful. We were home.

I've climbed my hill, settled in, created a home, and allowed my home to shape me. When I travel, I now consciously take *all* of me, including my restless humanity, on the journey.

WHAT ARE YOU WAITING FOR?

Explore your connections to places (and sense of place) by answering these questions:

1. What do places represent to you? Home, loss, new beginnings, freedom?
2. What does the phrase "geographical cure" signify to you?
3. What is important to you? A sense of community? Nature? Wide-open vistas? City life (the hustle and bustle, museums, restaurants)?
4. Describe a time you have attempted to use a place to escape. What were you looking for?

ESSAYS ON DISRUPTING THE ORDINARY

"Coming Home to Me" by Patricia Moeller

I love where I live, but it wasn't always this way. My valley (yes, I feel ownership for it in a way that is powerfully connected to all its inhabitants) is a source of support and comfort for me. Every time I return from vacation, I think, "Wow, thank God that I am home." The thankfulness comes not from the dislike of other places, but rather from the comfort of knowing that I choose to create my future anywhere I call home. I grew up in Alaska and felt confined, wanting more than anything to leave and one day be *free*.

At twenty-three, I finally escaped and found myself sailing for a year and a half down the inter-coastal waterway to the Bahamas. Money being the deciding factor, I came ashore in Ft. Lauderdale, Florida, only to find myself, six months later, skiing the slopes of Jackson Hole. I felt grounded in Jackson, at home—a feeling that I had never experienced. The Tetons became my higher power, like a motherly source of inspiration—constantly shifting and changing, although really always the same.

In what occurred as a stroke of bad luck, my boyfriend (now husband) needed to go back to Florida to continue his flight training. I reluctantly went with him, even though I desperately wanted to stay in the first place that really seemed like home.

After two years in Florida, two years in Maine, two years in Rhode Island, and two years in Colorado, I returned home to Wyoming. Strangely, my friends were all eight years older! Without the geographical changes and experiences, I would not be the person I am today. I have a master's degree, two amazing children (born in different states), sobriety, and a spiritual completeness that comes from finding oneself and coming full circle. It is strange that I had to leave a place to be able to come back.

In the coming back, however, I found who I am.

7

JACKPOT

For the love of money is a root of all kinds of evil. Some
people, in their eagerness to get rich, have wandered away
from the faith and caused themselves a lot of pain.
1 Timothy 6:10, (ISV)

Arguably, more than any other area, we are the most confused about money.

Money became my ticket to acceptance, an access to fitting in. Upon my return to Florida to live with my mother, I was to attend an exclusive private school, which promised to prepare me for college. All I could think about was wearing the *right* clothes. With renewed determination, I spent an entire afternoon trying on different outfits. I was sure I'd found it—light blue striped chinos, a button-down white blouse, and the cutest tan wedge sandals. I pulled into the parking lot in my sparkling white Chevy Chevette, feeling pretty proud.

My first glimpse of the campus included rows of BMWs, Mercedes and Cadillacs. In the distance were perfectly manicured lawns, a fountain, and a bell tower. Was this my new school or an elite country club? As I walked toward the buildings, cheerleaders talking together turned and laughed. Later I learned their verdict—tacky shoes. Wrong again! Those girls *clearly* had something I didn't.

Convinced that if I could buy the *right* outfits and fit in, everything would finally fall into place, I shopped. I would beg my mother to give me the credit card and spend hours in the mall picking out new clothes. This behavior followed me into adulthood. Plastic became the answer.

Layaway—what does that mean? I couldn't wait, I needed it *now*! I told myself I deserved it as I snuck my shopping bags into the house.

I never learned the value of earning the money I needed before I purchased what I wanted. I bought clothes I never wore. I became a helpless princess—a compulsive shopper who wanted the finer things in life but didn't believe she could earn the money to pay for them. I was waiting to hit the jackpot. I didn't believe I could create it for myself. I lived the fantasy that it would come from somewhere outside of me, so I didn't have to be responsible. In recovery, I saw that my behavior was rooted in my deep lack of self-worth. Only by conscious intervention could I begin changing my beliefs and actions.

> *We rarely think to question the financial*
> *concepts we believe in and follow.*
> Garrett B. Gunderson, *Killing Sacred Cows*

At a recent social gathering, a group of us explored our hidden beliefs about money. We allowed ourselves to answer the question unabashedly, "What does money mean to you?" The variety of responses was astonishing:

Freedom
Danger
Success
Fulfillment
Burden
Guilt
Excitement
Love
Security
Happiness

We went on to explore messages we have heard about money. Again the answers were across the board:

> Spend wisely.
> Treat yourself.
> Die broke.
> Money is scarce.
> Abundance is everywhere.
> Be a millionaire, but don't appear like one.
> Debt is bad.
> Invest in yourself.
> Don't be greedy.
> It's rude to talk about money.

I'm continually surprised how often I hear "money is the root of all evil," either directly coming from people's mouths or seeping into their speaking from undistinguished belief systems. Oddly, I hear it frequently from those on a spiritual path. They seem to believe, "I am so much closer to God now that I am broke," as if having money is incompatible with spirituality.

What *is* the root of our problematic relationship with money?

> Is money itself the problem?
> Is it our relationship to money?
> Is it our lack of trust in ourselves?

OUTSIDE LOOKING IN

Joan explained, "I came from a lower-middle-class family. Both my parents worked hard and provided for us the best they could. Every day after school, I babysat for the neighbors to earn extra money for my family. The school I attended had a lot of rich kids, some of whom were my friends. I didn't want to have my friends over to my house. Their houses were so much more fun. I shared a room with my sister, whereas many of my friends had suites the size of my entire house. We would swim in their pools, eat their exquisite food, and play croquet on their lawns. We played dress-up for hours, lost in the vast closets of their mothers, trying on clothes. Many of my friends were generous and let me take home 'extra' clothes they didn't wear. I started to resent that my family couldn't live like this. It didn't seem fair. I vowed to live the way my friends did. Being a good student anyway, I excelled in school, went to the top of my class, and went to law school on loans and a scholarship. After graduating law school and getting a job (with the help of my best friend's parents) at a top law firm, I started making more money each month than my father made in a year. I bought a penthouse apartment, wore the best clothes, and ate at the finest restaurants—only I wasn't happy. So I bought a fancier apartment, a new BMW, went on a trip to the Caribbean, and still I wasn't happy."

Her eyes filling with tears, Joan went on, "I finally realized the money wasn't going to make me happy! I saw I had been ashamed of the way I grew up, embarrassed by my working-class parents. I had been making all of it wrong—my family, my friends, myself, and most of all, the money *itself.* Coming from this place, there was no way I could be happy. After coming to terms with this and apologizing to my dear family, I realized I could choose to make money but not be driven by it. I realized there was nothing wrong with the money itself. What needed to change was my attitude towards money."

Dissatisfaction and unhappiness are the result when we search externally for the jackpot. I will be happy when I have (this much) money in the bank, when I am out of debt, when the economy turns around, when I make a certain amount per year. We fall into this trap when we reduce our self-worth to the amount of money we have or objects we own. Hitting the jackpot will make me and everything in my life all right. Right? No, unfortunately this is the illusion.

Waiting for the jackpot keeps us:

- Confused. We think money means things that it doesn't.
- Ashamed. We try to hide our financial situation from everyone, especially those closest to us. It's one of those "taboo" topics that we *don't* talk about.
- In Denial. Either we think our situation is worse than it actually is, or we pretend it's better.
- Dishonest. We spend money on things we can't afford and lie to ourselves.

These persistent questions keep us trapped:

- Why can't I do what I want?
- Why can't I live like *those* people (the "keeping up with the Joneses" phenomenon)?
- Why can't I have *that?*

And the deeper, largely unconscious beliefs driving us are:

- I am not enough.
- *Those* people are better than I am.
- There is not enough to go around, so I better get mine while I can.

Meanwhile, we *wait*. We wait to *have* enough. We wait to *be* enough.

SCARCITY

The pervasive fear that "there isn't enough" can lead us to the "Disease of More." More is better! Hoarding is a symptom of this "disease." Don't clean out the closet—just in case. Those who suffer from the "Disease of More" can no longer distinguish *wanting* from *needing* or *useful* from *obsolete*.

Sarah put it this way: "I never wanted to get rid of anything, especially my clothes. I would always think: I better save this outfit! What if my great-granddaughter (who hasn't yet been born) needs to dress as a gypsy for Halloween? So when my closets filled up, I took over the spare room. When that filled up, I filled up my garage. It went on and on like that. I was so afraid of giving anything away—what if I *needed* it? I finally saw the old, fear-driven beliefs that kept this behavior in place, and I could let go. Little by little, I started giving things away. One day I felt particularly free, and I rented a U-haul; and with the help of my friends cleared out all the clutter. I have never felt so free in my life! I was so inspired that I am starting a new career to assist others in doing the same!"

Changing old habits isn't always easy; even after drastically transforming my attitude and behavior around money, my husband gave me the nickname "Buy-in-Bulk Moeller." I nearly require a second vehicle for my trips to Costco. God forbid we run out of paper towels! An old friend asked me if I still fill my coffee cups to overflowing, and I had to respond, "Yes!" I don't want to give that one up … yet.

But I Want It!

Often we decide what we want based on what others have. On a trip to Los Angeles, I had the pleasure of being introduced to a closet full of dazzling Jimmy Choos. This closet was heaven with rows of beautifully crafted, stunningly gorgeous shoes. (Remember my shoe issue from high school?) Suddenly, my favorite pair of black sandals were *not enough*. I had to have Jimmy Choos! But my budget didn't support this craving. The wheels started turning: how could I get them? Did I have enough room on my credit card? Would my husband notice? The thought pattern felt all too familiar: it begins as a craving, becomes a longing and then an obsession which I disguise as a need. There will be no satisfaction until I have what I want! And I spend my way to my imaginary jackpot.

Media and advertising geniuses prey on our insecurities. "Feeling empty inside? Buy this, take this trip, you'll feel better. Try some retail therapy, and you'll be happy."

Many people still believe that "he who dies with the most toys wins." We may pretend we don't believe that anymore, thinking, "Oh, that's so 1980s," but underneath, we still look for the next hot, "have-to-have-it" thing. We want it all now—the newest cell phone, the smallest laptop. No waiting here! We want instant gratification—we want what we want when we want it.

Financial ignorance is costly. Studies show that the average person doesn't know the basics of money management. This level of denial can lead to the dangers of over-spending and accumulated (and non-productive) debt. Many people are heavily in debt; some are losing their homes.

Unfortunately, there are those who prey on our desire for money. Get-rich-quick schemes rarely deliver what they promise, but we continue to get sucked in.

A young couple I worked with bought it hook, line, and sinker. They had two small kids and another on the way, were self-employed, and wanted to make a difference for their family and their future. They were prime targets for a predatory investor scam. The grand promises of being able to retire through real estate "investments" blinded them, and they bought the fantasy. It was too good to be true. They lost everything.

A BALANCING ACT

Our basic needs are actually quite simple: air, food, water, and shelter (and love). We can categorize just about anything else as a "want." Unfortunately, our wants can become a bottomless pit. And let me be clear, *there is nothing wrong with wanting!* However, if we allow our wants to drive us, we have squandered our power, and we have abdicated control.

I did not act on my impulse that day in Los Angeles. However I did continue to want those Jimmy Choos. In this case, waiting paid off.

To celebrate the completion of writing this book, a group of my dear friends came together and bought me my very own pair. Did I need these shoes? No. Did they make me complete? No. But do I love having them and appreciate the generosity of my friends? You bet!

How and where we spend our money is a choice. Our spending remains within our control. We can live the fantasy of spending and spending our way to a higher standard of living, or we can live within our means.

In addition to choosing how we spend, we can also choose our financial perspective. We can view ourselves as victims, live in denial, pretend things aren't the way they are—or we can choose to accept what is and act accordingly. And from this foundation of acceptance, if we want more money we can create ways to acquire it.

The funny thing is that *money has no inherent meaning in itself.* It is only a piece of paper with green printing. It's who we become regarding money and the meanings we give it that make it something other than it is.

Like all areas, it's about balance. Rather than make ourselves wrong for wanting, we can accept the fact that we will always want, and that it's okay. Part of allowing ourselves to dream is to want something better for ourselves *and* for the world. However, if we continue to w*ant* our way out of the present moment, we have returned to waiting. We lose our freedom. Then the wanting has us as we wait forever for the elusive jackpot.

Practice

Start Wherever You Are:
Tell the entire truth to someone about your money beliefs, behaviors, issues, and concerns. Inventory what you have and what you don't have. Get clear on what is so.

Develop Your Own Wisdom:
Don't believe everything you hear or read about money. Take the time to educate yourself—don't blindly trust an "expert." Read *Killing Sacred Cows* by Garrett B. Gunderson.

WHAT ARE YOU WAITING FOR?

No matter where you are on the money scale, this is an opportunity to remove your head from the sand and see what's really happening.

1. What beliefs, concepts, and stories do you have about money? What does money mean to you?
2. What were the messages you received about money growing up?
3. What messages about money do you perpetuate?
4. Do you let yourself want? When does wanting become waiting for the jackpot?
5. What anticipated or hoped for financial shift has you waiting to get what you want and be who you want to be?

ESSAYS ON DISRUPTING THE ORDINARY

"The Gift of Failure" by Dave Fichter

Almost twenty years ago, I experienced a series of shocks brought on by financial problems that pummeled me into submission. These "life tremblers" began with a call from a local travel agent who threatened to have my wife arrested for grand larceny and ended with the discovery that my house had been in foreclosure without my knowledge. Along the way came the less-shocking revelations of liens imposed by the IRS for failure to pay taxes and penalties that I had never known about, loans from friends never repaid, and numerous occurrences of electric, phone, and cable services being shut off.

Aside from putting an enormous—and ultimately fatal—strain on my marriage, these experiences forced me to confront the truth about myself: I had been running from responsibility, not just financial, but in all other ways. Out of this humiliation I was given the gift of humility, and with that the humbleness to ask for help. It began with my seeing a psychotherapist, who suggested my wife and I enter marriage counseling, which in turn led to my admission that I was an alcoholic. From that darkest of days, where I seemed to be sinking into a bottomless hole of despair, my feet struck something solid, and I began to rebuild my life on newer and more lasting principles. I got sober with the help of a growing support network of people, like those in my twelve-step program. I developed my spiritual life—*note*, not *religious life;* I began to recover, not just from alcoholism, but also in all aspects of my life. I learned how to take responsibility for my actions, which meant accepting whatever consequences came from them, and to face my fears—no matter how insurmountable they seemed—and to walk through them.

As I rebuilt my life on this bedrock, I made a stark and unflinching assessment of my values and what was most important to me. There were casualties from this inventory, among them my marriage and my career of twenty-five years—things which I believed *defined* me. I tenaciously hung onto them while ignoring any information that might threaten these false stanchions of my life. But when finally free of these illusions, along with a great many material things that went with them, I felt lighter and freer. I vowed to hold on to this newfound freedom no matter what.

But it's funny how our best *intentions* so often are forgotten. From my spare and more flexible life grew new opportunities, like new sprouts from cleared underbrush, and I seized them. I soon found myself possessing far more than I had given up—proof (I thought) that my Higher Power was rewarding me for my efforts. From that belief I soon came to believe that my rewards were due solely to my own efforts, and that as long as I tried harder, I would reap more. Somewhere along the line I became possessed by my possessions, and beset by the same fear that had brought me to my knees almost two decades before. I deferred or avoided entirely any consequences or accountability of my actions, only to see them loom up again, bigger and scarier as the stakes increased. Finally I came face to face with the truth: *recovery and growth are not destinations;* instead they are journeys that go on for a lifetime.

I sit here writing this, again humbled. I have come to realize that our traditional view of success does not fit the life I have or describe the miracle that it is. I've discovered the best lessons and biggest rewards come out of admitting defeat (and acknowledging "what is"), but *only* if we don't give up. Defeat and failure can be gifts, but we need the courage to open them. I wish many "gifts" to be placed under your tree, along with the courage to unwrap them.

8

JACK AND THE BEANSTALK

Barn's burnt down ... now I can see the moon.
Masahide

John Lennon said, "Life is what happens to you while you're busy making other plans." Life happens, loss happens, illness happens. People we love die, and ultimately (of course) we all die. When loss, illness, or tragedy strike, it is easy to ask "why?" But the more important questions are, "Who are we going to *be* in the midst of it all? How will we act? What will we do?"

Once again, how we respond to these life events has its roots in childhood. Many of us developed coping skills which don't serve us in the long run. Some of us even turn these events into *dramas*. Drama makes us feel alive and passionate. For some of us, life can seem dull without it. Drama *is* part of the full range of human experience. Yet when we take it to extremes, it becomes another way we wait to live.

ADDICTED TO DRAMA

Bethany admitted, "I never thought I was someone who liked drama. I always thought I just got the short end of the stick. My mother left (and never came back) when I was 9 and I was understandably devastated. I remember having a lot of anxiety. My father had three of us to raise. I was the only girl, and I helped him as best I could. My oldest brother started using drugs and got in trouble at school. Even though I did as much as I could for my family, it didn't seem like I got enough attention. I started getting sick a lot. It seemed like I would catch every cold or flu that went through school. I remember *loving* the attention I got on those days. I would eagerly wait for my dad to make me chicken soup and tuck me in bed after reading my favorite book, *Jack and the Beanstalk.* I felt loved and safe.

"I don't know when I first started wanting to be sick so I could get attention. It was part of my life for so long. I had a series of minor illnesses. I became the person always going to the doctor. I always left feeling better, skipping along with my bag of medicine. I would feel energized for a while. My family and friends were worried, telling me to rest and take it easy.

"One day I attended a lecture and heard someone share a story that felt eerily similar to mine. The speaker described her behavior as an 'addiction to drama.' I didn't like what I heard. She went on to say that although she had a lot of illness throughout her life, and she made many of her symptoms worse by the way she lived. She used illness as an excuse to wait for others to take care of her and to avoid being responsible for her life. She thought the only way she could get the love and attention she craved was to be ill. After learning how to ask for what she wanted, many of her symptoms improved.

"For the next week, I reflected on my life. I saw much of my behavior was based on this decision I made in childhood. I saw how I waited and longed for love and attention that I thought I was lacking. "

Chuckling, Bethany goes on to say, "I thought back to Jack and that beanstalk he kept climbing. The giant was coming, and he *finally* realized the danger. I realized that I didn't have to keep climbing my proverbial beanstalk looking for attention and love. I was finally ready to stop waiting for someone to 'fix' me. I let my behavior go—I cut down the beanstalk!

"Sometimes I still want to take a ride to the wild side and become dramatic, but most of the time I choose peace. Still, when I have 'symptoms,' I can't always tell if I'm I really tired or simply in a funky mood. Am I getting a cold, or do I just need to sleep? Am I seeking attention? Or am I just avoiding something I need to do that I don't want to?

"I can gently laugh at myself for the occasional enjoyment I get from being on the doctor's table and having people tell me what to do. It's the ultimate in being taken care of. For a moment, it lets me return to the feeling of the snugness of the womb. I don't have to judge or resist my drama. I can observe it, accept it, and not let it run my life. And I have found peace."

ONCE UPON A TIME, I WAS A SUN GODDESS

In 1996, I was diagnosed with melanoma. One day, I noticed a flat, small, white spot on my forearm and showed my doctor. He told me, "That's nothing, your moles are boring, don't worry about it." Over the summer, this white spot turned pink. After moving to Colorado, I went to a new doctor. This honey of a man said, "We should take it off." I didn't think a lot about it, but a week later, the call came. "It's melanoma … cancer … we have to operate soon."

I knew nothing about melanoma at the time. Equating being tan with looking good, I had always been a sun worshipper. In high school we would lie on white sheets and coat ourselves with baby oil to fry like bacon. I burned frequently and spent nights covered in Noxzema®, which took the red and the sting away. Once I covered my burns with loose tea leaves because a friend had told me my redness would turn tan, but instead the leaves stuck on my raw, bubbly skin.

I was one of the lucky ones—we caught my melanoma early. People die horrible deaths from melanoma. I love this doctor; he saved my life. It was only after my surgery that I really got scared, afraid the cancer might come back. So I changed my behavior. No more obsession with being tan—it was time to embrace my paleness. Long-sleeved shirts, a lot of sunscreen, and hats. For a while I felt sorry for myself.

ME, A DRAMA QUEEN?

I started a new job during the time of my melanoma surgery. After a few absences from work, a co-worker questioned whether my health "issues" would get in the way of my job. I was offended. How could she ask such a thing? I didn't want to be sick! What happened to me was *not* a choice! How dare she!

A few years later, I attended a week-long retreat where a counselor raised the same question. This time I couldn't ignore it. I had developed a pattern. I would work like crazy, go and go, run and run, and then collapse with a cold or the flu, which *finally* let me rest. I was waiting for something outside of myself to give me the permission to stop. Like Bethany, I was climbing the beanstalk over and over again, looking for something that wasn't there—someone or something that would take care of me so I didn't have to.

I never thought I enjoyed (or created) drama, but now I see I did. For many years, I used illness as a way out. I began by falling off a horse to avoid performance anxiety. I became a walking train wreck so people would notice me. And it worked. At the time, I didn't consciously make the connection, yet I learned how to get the attention I craved. Also, I reasoned that if I was sick, people wouldn't expect much of me. They would let me off the hook and take care of me. My ailments provided an excuse to avoid any risk of failure.

Although I did not consciously choose to develop Melanoma, I saw that I still used illness to avoid being responsible for my life. Throughout the years, I have had other things to deal with—the death of dear friends, my own fertility struggles, pregnancy losses, and thyroid issues, to name a few. Each time "life happens," I have an opportunity to choose who I am going to be. It's like a car slightly out of alignment. When I take my hands off the wheel, it slowly drifts off course. So I keep a *gentle* grip on the wheel and continue on my journey. I practice awareness and compassion with myself and others. I have learned to look for the gift in all of it and inquire, "What am I supposed to see? What do I need to learn?"

POWER IN LIFE

How we deal with illness or loss is obviously a sensitive subject. I am certainly not suggesting that all who suffer secretly wish for drama. I include these stories as another point of access to see where we might be out of balance or lack power—another area where we wait to live. Now I gently coach my clients to look for signs of their drama approaching. Often when we are not well or when we are dealing with loss, our energy level, focus, and concentration dip. We can't think straight. The world doesn't look as sunny. This is prime breeding ground for drama! And this is the time to draw on all of our support, to use all of our tools, to practice what we have learned.

What Are You Waiting For?

We are perfectly imperfect. We are fine the way we are, even when we have barriers to our natural self-expression. Some barriers are more serious and debilitating than others. The trick is to see them, acknowledge them, and find out how to make peace with them so they don't control your life. Answer the following questions to help you along the way:

1. What do you have difficulty accepting in yourself?
2. What is your proverbial beanstalk? Are you willing to stop climbing it, to cut it down?
3. Where do you create drama in your life?
4. Has something happened in your past that you haven't let go, that you are waiting to handle, that even now does not feel like a lesson or a gift?
5. Can you be willing to see the gift? If so, what is it?

Essays on Disrupting the Ordinary

"Coming Back to Life" by David Cottrell

Finishing up my run, I was going to walk the last quarter mile back to the house. Then my brother-in-law and I were off for a fishing trip on the Rhode Island coast, and tomorrow he was getting married. Slowly, I started feeling a tightening in my left hindquarter, quickly followed by debilitating pain in my low back. I was afraid I was going to have to crawl the remaining distance to the house.

I had started having back pain in high school, but I would always recover within a day or two. This event started a series of debilitating episodes in which I would be relegated to the couch or the bed for a week at a time. My quality of life deteriorated, and I stopped participating in events that I used to love in order to avoid the pain. I felt sorry for myself most of the time and was easily annoyed and irritable. In 2005, seven years after that day in Rhode Island, I started looking for a surgeon. Then something unexpected happened.

I registered myself into a weekend-long course that I didn't really want to take. But it was a requirement of some other training that I *did* want to take, so there I was. The course dealt with looking at the things that hold us back in life and get in the way of who we could be. During the course, I saw a few startling things. First, I realized I had been using my back pain to get attention. Now if you had asked me, "Hey David, do you like the attention you get from being in pain all the time?" I would have called you a name and told you that you were nuts. I discovered *that* was the hard truth. Additionally, I would use the pain and my bad attitude to punish people around me (like my wife) so I didn't have to be responsible for my life in general. I was a victim. As the course went on, I discovered why.

As a child, there was always some drama going on in my home. Usually, I could get someone to feel sorry for me and give me some love if I was hurt, sad or remorseful. It *had* worked for me, so I had carried the behavior forward into my adult life where it clearly no longer served me.

After the weekend course, the pain slowly subsided. Something about becoming responsible for my behavior transformed me physically, and *I no longer needed surgery*. In fact, last year, I was able to go skiing for the first time in eight years. That is not to say that I don't have pain—I do. But I have it, it does not have me.

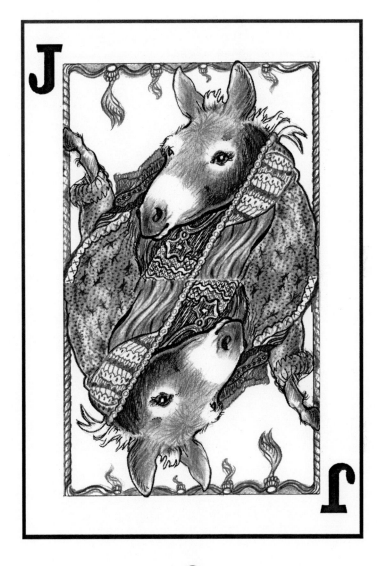

9
JACKASS

Rule 62: Don't take yourself so damn seriously.
from *Twelve Steps and Twelve Traditions: Alcoholics Anonymous*

When the gigantic, muddy paw print in the middle of my freshly printed manuscript doesn't remind me of the simple perfection of life, I am being a jackass.

My husband and I share our lives with two Rhodesian Ridgebacks, one ornery tabby cat, and an old (but full of beans) Thoroughbred horse. Our animals are often my greatest teachers—they are my "significance barometer." They assist me in seeing when I am off track, when I have forgotten the joy of the moment. They show me the profound gift of the simple things in life.

One of the results of being that little girl who tried so hard to get it "right" (and then continued to fail to do so) was that I became *significant* about life. Everything, from doing well in school to achieving the latest fashion trend *mattered*—and I mean that it mattered a lot when I didn't *get it right*. Although I am often told I have a "joyous heart," I frequently get caught up in being oh-so-serious. When I get like this, I forget that life is a joyous adventure. I tell myself that if only I could get it right, my life would be great, and I would be completely happy. This is another way that we wait—we make the insignificant *significant*, and that stalls us from growing, moving forward. By surrounding myself with animals, I have a constant reminder of what is really important to me: being present, unconditional love, deep connections, quiet, and peace. My animals help ground me, help me remember the path I am on.

I host a weekly radio show and every week (without fail) I get nervous the day before the show. I start doubting myself, and for a moment I forget that I actually enjoy doing it. I easily slip into being a *significant jackass*. One of my practices for "snapping out of it" is to engross myself in the world of my dogs.

Roscoe, the younger Ridgeback, teaches me the pleasure of being happy. In fact, he *is* happiness. We have a game we play for pure joy. I am transported as I observe him ripping and tearing up and down the hill, over logs, twisting and turning through bushes while he narrowly averts any obstacles in his way. We yell "run around"—not exceptionally eloquent—but it keeps him going at a velocity that is both inspiring and terrifying.

When my attitude calls for a quick adjustment, all I need to do snuggle down on the floor with one or both of them and listen to them snore with contentment. I arise, refreshed and reconstituted as an easygoing human being, the person I want to be as I interview my radio show guests.

I practice this in other areas where I tend to become significant. While I write, it's especially crucial that I keep my significance scale close to zero; therefore, I periodically stare at my dogs while they sleep on their giant feather bed in the sunny spot by the window. When not dozing, they gaze out at the view, seeming to meditate, but more likely scouting chipmunks. These dogs know how to enjoy life. They lie around in the sun on the deck or under a tree in the dirt. We cook for them, we rub their bellies, and they wag their tails, fart, and groan. Although Dog is God spelled backwards, it actually spells love. Pure love.

A recent Harris Poll said nearly two-thirds of Americans have a pet, and close to nine out of ten of them consider their pets to be members of the family. Most pet owners form connections with their animals that are life-altering and enhancing.

Lessons in Unconditional Love

As a newly married couple, we decided it was time to have a puppy. Many choices faced us—how would we determine the right variety? Then one day I met Rhett. I walked unsuspectingly into our local vet's office, and there he was—one-hundred pounds of solid muscle, a deep reddish brown, a gorgeous square head. A true hunk. I begged my husband to come see him. When we arrived, we waited for a few moments until two majestic creatures strolled in. Rhett, headed straight for David, crawled up and across his lap, went to sleep, and farted with contentment.

We were hooked. After carefully interviewing breeders, we finally brought home our first, precious child, the love of our lives, a seven-week-old Rhodesian Ridgeback puppy. We named him Jaxson. He was cute, sweet, and tinier than our cat. We couldn't believe our good fortune. We took him everywhere to introduce him to this beautiful world.

Then he ate his first—and my favorite—pair of shoes. I was fuming. But there he was, wagging his tail, staring up at me with his caramel eyes, black muzzle, and wrinkled brow. At that moment I knew how insignificant those shoes were compared to my love for this dog. My capacity for acceptance proved greater than I ever imagined before.

Most mornings, Jaxson waits for me to get up. We descend the stairs together for our first cup of coffee. If I pause, he does as well. Together we wait on the rise to be greeted by my husband.

Now he's gray around the eyes, slightly slower and stiffer, but still a puppy at heart. He lowers his head and charges his ninety-five pounds straight into us. His ears fall to the sides and his head drops down as he crashes towards us.

The depth of our adoration for this particular animal is astounding. As Jaxson grows older, he becomes sweeter and more connected to us. My heart hurts because I know he won't be with us forever. So I consciously soak up all the precious moments, cherish them, and feel grateful and blessed.

REMEMBER RULE 62

My ambition in life is to someday be the person my dog thinks I am.
Emily Maughan

My dogs remind me of who I am when I forget Rule 62, and I take myself too seriously. If you were to visit my house, my dogs wouldn't care if you are a doctor or a janitor, a mom or a nun, a famous author or the President—they only want to sniff your butt.

The truth is, when I noticed I was waiting for Jack, I realized I was acting as if Jack was *the* answer—that somehow knowing him would provide something that I thought I was missing internally. He might give me access to a world that I only dreamed about. I had placed him on a pedestal, and when we put someone on a pedestal, where does that leave us? Taking this a step further, when we place someone on a pedestal, we develop unrealistic expectations of them—we set them up to fall and to fail.

We can be such jackasses! We waste time by elevating one human being over another. And we waste time *and* cause harm when we do the opposite by thinking we are better than someone else. We all come into this world the same way. We are all made of flesh and blood. Our insides are the same—it's only our individual expression of our humanity that differs. When we believe we are inferior (or superior) to one another, we lose our connection. But none of this is wrong; it's simply us being human. However, if we are aware of it, we can choose not to do it, not elevate, and not set up the failure of both ourselves and the person we admire.

> If we are open and willing, animals can teach us to be better humans. We can learn gently to allow our imperfections (and those of others).

Animals can inspire us to be less busy, more present, less worried, more joyful, and more passionate about life. They will never judge us for the things we do or don't do. Animals don't complain. They don't create drama. Their type of waiting is patience personified. Their view of the world is immediate. They don't regret the past, fear the future, or take themselves "so damn seriously." And they teach us to be excited about the little things, the simple pleasures in life—dried dog food for dinner (again) never seems to lose its magic.

WHAT ARE YOU WAITING FOR?

1. What does your connection with animals mean to you?
2. Where do *you* find yourself taking life too seriously?
3. Where are you being a jackass?
4. Where do you love unconditionally? Where do you not?

ESSAYS ON DISRUPTING THE ORDINARY

"The Three-legged Dog" by Gayle George

A three-legged dog saved my life. I never knew her name. The dog had no pedigree, no owner, and no home. She roamed the courtyard of an apartment complex I moved into just before the holidays. She was always there—wild, but not menacing—with sad, runny eyes and an odd kind of limp. By the looks of her wounds, this dog had barely survived a serious car accident and received no medical attention. She was only alive by the grace of God and the kindness of strangers. It was a catch phrase I had begun using to describe my own existence in those days. She would soon help me change that reality for good.

I was stranded in Mozambique, a poor southern African country, with no money, no real prospects, and no return ticket to the states. After nearly two years of trying to establish myself in the region, I had run out of answers. Things shifted the night I dreamed the three-legged dog entered my apartment to watch *The Oprah Winfrey Show*. She held a tattered rag doll in her mouth which was made into the likeness of an African woman. Oprah was reaching toward the dog, saying, 'Let it go. You can let it go. Give it to me.' Reluctantly, the dog released the doll. As it fell from her mouth, the dog's mangled hindquarter began to heal. A renewed back leg stretched down toward the floor. When the transformation was complete, the dog stood triumphantly on all fours. She became taller, her eyes cleared, and her coat shone bright and new.

I woke up feeling relieved and energized. The three-legged dog was a sign for me to let go of what was not working and focus on creating the life I wanted to live instead. Once I made the decision to go home and start over, everything began to move with Godspeed.

The three-legged dog reminded me of the choice we have in every moment. We can focus our energies on surviving with things that may handicap us physically, emotionally, or spiritually; or we can choose to thrive in spite of them. It takes a tremendous amount of effort to change patterns, lifestyles, affiliations, relationships, or situations that no longer serve us, but the courage and the commitment to do so is always rewarded exponentially. The three-legged dog inspired me to venture beyond the courtyard of limitations where I had confined myself. She showed me how to let go of my wounded existence and embrace the discomfort associated with progress and healing. For the insight she provided, helping me choose to walk a little taller, I am forever grateful.

PART THREE:

SPIRIT

Row, row, row your boat,
Gently down the stream.
Merrily, merrily, merrily, merrily,
Life is but a dream
Eliphalet Oram Lyte

10
JACK IN THE BOX

What we are looking for is doing the looking.
Sufi saying

I have heard the way to train fleas is first to place them in a jar and then put on the lid. The fleas will jump repeatedly and hit the lid as they attempt to escape. After about twenty minutes, the fleas tire of hitting the lid and learn not to jump as high. If you remove the lid, the fleas will continue to jump at the lower height and never break out. They adjust to the limitation of the lid on the jar and stop trying to escape, *even* when the circumstances change. They don't escape because they *believe* they can't.

We are like the fleas. We live with the belief that a lid exists—even when it isn't there. However, in our case, instead of a jar, we limit ourselves by living life in a box.

Our searching, waiting, and looking outside ourselves for answers *is* actually living life in a box.

How We Construct Our Boxes

Our eagerness for certainty boxes us in.
Mark Epstein, *Going on Being*

As I have described throughout this book, I created strategies to shield myself from pain and uncertainty. Although I thought I was staying safe, I was actually restricting my experience and self-expression. That moment in third grade when I felt so embarrassed about pronouncing *Chicago* as *Chick-a-go,* I vowed to avoid the risk of judgment and decided never to raise my hand again. I unconsciously created a box, and subsequently fortified the walls of the box with each decision I made.

As we go through life, we react to events and make decisions based on the meaning we give to our experiences. From there, consciously or unconsciously, these opinions, strategies and views influence how our lives will go. Something we label "bad" happens to us and we say, "I won't let *that* happen again."

On the other extreme, when something we label "good" happens, we attempt to ensure a positive outcome by repeating the positive action. For instance, we wear a blue suit and give a successful presentation at work and from then on believe we *need* to wear that suit whenever we want to succeed again.

These attempts to avoid the bad and repeat the good become life-defining behavior patterns. Inside our box, accustomed as we are to our view, we can't see the boundaries we put around our range of experience. We live cautiously, protecting ourselves and "playing it safe." We want to know what's going to happen; therefore, we organize and compartmentalize life so we will know what to expect. Our boxes provide a false sense of certainty in their limited spheres. They give the illusion of order and provide the hope that we are ensconced in a womb of safety.

ALL BOXED IN

A box is everything that limits us. Often we think it is something outside of us, but it is actually our internal process—our view, our opinions, our position, our thoughts, and our feelings.

Boxes come in many different sizes and shapes, and they can encompass many areas of life. To further clarify the constraints of living life in a box—and to think outside the box—contemplate the following:

- **The Box of Jealousy and Envy:** When someone close to us succeeds, we may truly want to be happy for them, but instead we may feel discouraged and wonder, "What about me? I want that!"

  A friend who is an incredibly talented artist had her work featured in a national magazine. I congratulated her and expressed how excited I was for her. She was shocked and whispered to me, "You're the only person who has said that to me." People in her life felt threatened by her success.

  On some level, we all feel envy and jealousy. We fall into the trap of this box when we falsely believe that the success of others takes something away from us, that there isn't enough to go around.

- **The Box of Perfection:** We each have our own view of perfection and often measure ourselves and others against this unrealistic ideal. We then become trapped in the quest for perfection, especially when we try to meet these impossible standards.

- **The Box of Comparison:** When we compare ourselves to others, it's easy to come up short, because few things are equal. Others may have had advantages of which we are not aware. When we compare ourselves, we could mistakenly believe, "They have some quality I don't," or even worse, turn our judgment inward and think, "I must be defective."

- **The Box of Time:** "I don't have enough time." How often do we hear ourselves saying just that? Yet we live with the illusion that *someday* we will have enough time and get everything done. This is the most basic trap of "waiting for Jack." The truth is that all we have is now. And as long as we are alive, we will never get *everything* done.

- **The Box of "Should":** We deceive ourselves with our ideas of how we, life, and others *should* be. This is often called "The Tyranny of the Should," a concept developed by the late personality theorist Karen Horney. Similar to the "Box of Perfection," we measure how we should be against external and internal ideals. And taking it a step further, we hold the underlying belief that if the world were the way *we* think it should be, everything would be okay. We would be happy, successful, and safe. Any time we find ourselves saying (or thinking) "I should" or "they should," that could be our warning signal that we are living in the "Box of Should."

- **Box of Rules:** Our addiction to certainty makes us invent and adopt rules. Rules are *authoritative principles which exist to guide behavior or action.* Many rules, such as laws and traffic codes, are clearly necessary. This box contains the rules about how *we think* we need to behave—the rules we made up ourselves and then act as if they are "true." As adults, we may think we left our old fears behind. Not so. Our fears continue to influence our behavior. We tell ourselves, "Don't make waves. Don't rock the boat. Don't upset the apple cart. Be good, be polite, be nice. Follow the rules. Stay safe!" We now have the opportunity to uncover the rules that run our lives. Living by self-created rules eliminates a whole range of potential experiences—things that could enhance life. If we stay safe and small, life will pass us by. As I have heard over the years, "We will die with our potential intact."

- **Pandora's Box:** How often do we think and say to ourselves or others, "I wouldn't do that." We fear that our actions may potentially open the door to harm or malevolent forces, so we play it safe and keep the lid closed.

- **Box of Spirituality:** This really could be called the box of "False Spirituality" or "Ego," because true spirituality has no limitations. I include this box because I have heard so many refer to it over the years. It is based on the belief we have a hole within us that needs to be filled—implying something is wrong or something within is missing. For many people with addictions, this is a common belief. The idea being we could fill the hole with something positive, like spirituality. But is this hole really there? If you think it exists, try to locate it! Nothing is missing, but we *feel* like it is.

Another pitfall of this box is the eternal search for the next spiritual experience—endlessly seeking those moments when everything makes sense, when time stops and we feel peaceful or at one with the universe. In his book *After the Ecstasy, the Laundry,* (another of my favorite Jacks) Jack Kornfield writes, "these [spiritual] experiences are more common than you know, and not far away. There is one further truth, however: They don't last. Our realizations and awakenings show us the reality of the world, and they bring transformation, but they pass."

Practice

Notice the Boxes:

Take a new look at an area of your life. Inquire as to where you may be boxed in. Ask yourself: What do you believe to be true about that area? Why do you believe it to be true? Is it possible it's not true? Are you willing to consider another view?

IT'S TIME TO WAKE UP

When we live life in a box, we stay on autopilot, convinced we clearly see it all. Our eyes may see, but our minds filter out what doesn't fit with our beliefs, views, and opinions, our vision obscured by the confines of our box.

Waking up to where we are boxed in is an ongoing process. When I realize I have been living in a box, suddenly everything is clear! I experience the possibilities and the vastness of life. As I move forward, I unconsciously begin to create walls again. This is part of the normal human cycle—we resist change and crave certainty. We have trained ourselves not to jump (remember the fleas) in order to stay safe and comfortable. Consider that all we *can* count on is:

> Nothing is solid or predictable.
> Nothing will stay the same.
> Nothing stays constant.
> Everything is in flux.
> There are no guarantees.

As Marcus Aurelius Antoninus wrote, "The Universe is change; our life is what our thoughts make it." Many of us have *hoped* life was different! Hope can be the lock that keeps us in the box. As long as we are hopeful, we will never let ourselves completely be who we are, where we are, or when we are. Hope can be what keeps us searching, looking outside ourselves for the answer, and waiting for Jack.

Some examples of how we indulge in hope and develop the habit of waiting are:

> I have hope for the future … it's got to be better than now.
> I hope everything will work out, eventually.
> I hope the next book I read, the next course I take, the next coach I hire will be the one who can make it all fall into place.
> I hope one day I will arrive and I can relax.
> I hope Jack e-mails me back …

As Mark Epstein wrote in *Going on Being*, "We experience the world through the filter of our minds." We think we are seeing clearly, but we only see within the confines of the boxes we've constructed. We think our perception is reality, and we call it our "circumstances." As long as we blame our circumstances, we have no power. When we become responsible for the boxes we have created, we then have true power.

To be free, we must release our attachment to our view of how life is and to our hope that it will be different. This is difficult—we love our *perception* of reality. But when we see the box for what it is and take responsibility for the walls we have constructed something *new* is possible.

Living in hope is not living in the moment—it is the ultimate in waiting. To give up hope and be willing to be in the unknown requires courage. It is the beginning of breaking free.

WHAT ARE YOU WAITING FOR?

1. Where are you living your life in a box?
2. How do your boxes limit your experience of life?
3. What are you willing to give up? Are you willing to give up your view of reality just to see what happens? Look for opportunities, they are *everywhere!*
4. Where do you use hope as an excuse not to live your life fully? Another way to look at this is—where are you hopeful yet not taking the action that will create what you *say* you want?

11
YOU DON'T KNOW JACK

Don't know is very important. "What am I?" Don't know … "Where is my mind?" Don't know … "When I die, where do I go?" Don't know … And actually, you really don't know, in the deepest, truest sense. And it is very important to look into that.
Zen Master Seung Sahn (1927-2004)

W^{hat} would be possible if you were willing to let go of your need to know?

Most of us don't like being in the unknown. It frightens us. We incessantly search for answers and wait for the truth. But once we find and identify the truth, it may no longer qualify as truth. When we define a concept, we also confine it, forcing it to remain fixed within our description. The "truth" then becomes limited to our view, our opinion, and our position.

The more we demand certainty, the further we are from finding it. When we become willing to stop waiting for certainty, we open ourselves to the unknown, which may be frightening, but can lead to new places, people, and ideas. As we learn to let go, there may be claw marks where we were holding on, but on the other side we can find freedom.

MY NEED TO KNOW

When my parents announced their divorce, it felt catastrophic and was a complete surprise to me. Suddenly, all I thought was certain no longer was. The family I thought would always be there no longer existed. The rug got pulled out from under me. My eight-year-old mind decided I needed to know everything in order to be prepared for other looming disasters.

I developed the need to know, the need to find the truth. I reasoned if I had only known about my parents' problems, things might have turned out differently; I could have prevented the divorce. I developed the erroneous belief that if I could just figure it all out, everything would fall into place. I could stop waiting. Life would return to normal—I would feel a sense of certainty, peace would reign in my world. I could put my family back together and everything would be okay.

Not surprisingly, my two favorite subjects in college were Art History and Psychology. In both disciplines, I loved the "search for truth" that seemed hidden just below the surface. When I finally let go of my obsessive need to know, I found myself experiencing life rather than trying to figure it out or control it. I realized that the rug pulled out from under me *never* existed. The false notion that there was a rug at all was simply my demand for certainty.

> True freedom begins with letting go of certainty. Once we *know,* we lose our ability to perceive what *is.* To challenge all we *think* we know—including our ideas about ourselves and others— allows something new to emerge. When we learn we are more than our thoughts, feelings, opinions, and circumstances, a new world can arise.

BE A BEGINNER

To let go of knowing is to practice "beginner's mind." Beginner's mind is the art of seeing everything fresh, without past constraints or future concerns. It's the art of being present.

To practice beginner's mind, we must step back and release what we *think* we know. Despite what we have achieved, learned, and acquired, we must be willing to let go of all that and see the world from a fresh perspective. We must give up what we believe and keep giving it up.

By practicing beginner's mind, we can actually enjoy the journey. We can give up trying to get somewhere. We can appreciate each moment and clearly see the richness of life as if for the first time.

As many Buddhist teachers say:

> If you're drinking tea, simply drink tea.
> If you're reading the newspaper, simply read the newspaper.
> If you're drinking tea and reading the newspaper, simply drink tea and read the newspaper.

Whatever you are doing ... do that!

Often we move through life half-awake with the heaviness of our views and opinions, and we don't even know we aren't present.

Practice

Seeing Objectively:
After you finish reading this "practice," stop and look around. Pick an object and try to observe it without having thoughts about it. See how long it lasts—how long your mind will stay clear.

It's difficult, isn't it? It is challenging to quiet our busy minds. Most of us are not aware of the constant mind chatter. It's been going on without respite for so long. We sort and classify and place every thought within the contexts we create. In our minds, we think we know how everything should go and how people should be. We wait for life to line up the way we think it should, but we do this unconsciously. As we live our lives, we look at the objects, people, and places surrounding us and immediately form opinions about them. We have no idea the extent to which we sort, classify, and judge.

Practice

Awareness:
Observe yourself. Notice what you're doing. Examine your automatic thoughts. Simply observe.
In every situation, with every person you encounter, ask yourself:

> Am I seeing *newly* or am I seeing from *the past*—through the veils of my preconceptions, thoughts, and opinions? Am I seeing things as they really are?

Take a fresh look at people, places, and things that are familiar to you.

MOMENTS

Recently, my husband and I spent an evening with our two glorious goddaughters, something we don't do often enough. The four of us went to a fast-food restaurant and since I had already eaten, I had the opportunity just to be with our little group and to observe.

The experience was extraordinary—simple and enchanting. I soaked up *everything* and felt wide awake. First I observed the restaurant itself—the corrugated metal walls, the smooth cement floor, and the contrasting colors. Then I turned my attention to the two magical creatures, our goddaughters, eating their meals and giggling. Then I watched the crinkles around my husband's blue eyes as he delighted in the company of the girls. Then I observed the other patrons in the restaurant—talking and laughing or silent and alone, meeting my eyes or looking away. Time slowed down. I experienced life without any filters or boxes as though my senses were newly born.

I was able to experience space, to hear the quiet. I was able to turn off the running commentary that is constantly in the background of my mind. I could stop assessing, judging, and putting everything in a box. I lost my mind and came to my senses, as Fritz Perls says.

I flourish in those moments, the mystical moments, when for a flash I can see the matrix of life. For me, like many others, immersion in music often creates those sensations. I lose myself and time slows. I feel alert and alive. Another such moment occurred at a concert of a band I love named Face. They are all-vocal, with no instruments and pure talent. Their music, attitudes, style, and sound speak to me.

The late summer sun was just beginning to set behind the stage. Beams of light framed these six intriguing and charismatic men. Their voices floated and danced through the crisp air. Seeing them perform that evening was a peak experience—the perfect combination of the beauty of a Colorado summer evening, music I love, and the band's energy and enthusiasm. I soaked it up, bathed in the glory, and felt grateful for such an extraordinary night.

I thought, "Yes, *this* is a moment I'll remember. I will sustain this glory. It will stay with me!" But the next day, I woke up and the crispness of the memory was already blurry. It had faded into the distance of the past.

When I encounter these moments, I crave more. However, when I look relentlessly for them, they elude me. If I ease up and stop pressing, they frequently appear. They're all around me in simple things. I see them in the shimmer of sunlight on a green leaf as I glance out my window, in the dappled shadows dancing on the ground as the wind roars through the pine trees. I just have to stop searching and let them arise.

For a long time, I feared life was passing me by. Since I couldn't recall some moments in detail, I thought I had missed them. I worried that, at the end of my life, I would look back and realize I hadn't lived fully enough. I would regret not having children, not being a good enough friend, not seeing enough of the world, not being grateful.

Then I saw that dwelling on all these concerns lands me back in waiting, which prohibits me from experiencing *this* moment. In any moment, I have a choice. I can mourn the passing of the moment or I can be in the now.

> What if those moments we do remember are enough and what we experienced is what we were supposed to experience?
>
> What if each moment is sufficient in itself?

All that really matters is the present moment. Everything else is just a memory, or a thought about that memory, or a construct of some imagined future. The past is gone, whether we remember it in vivid or sketchy detail. It is gone. All we have is *this* moment. And in the moment of the end of life, all we will have is the now of *that* moment.

What does it mean to miss a moment? It means nothing. We can let go of both the judgment that we missed something *and* that we missed anything at all.

DON'T BELIEVE EVERYTHING YOU THINK

If you believe everything you think, you are in trouble. Supposedly the average thinker has 15,000 thoughts a day, while a deep thinker has 50,000 thoughts per day. However, many thoughts repeat the same primary themes: various combinations of "something's wrong with me," "something's wrong with you," or "something's wrong with the world."

Wisdom is what is left when we run out of personal opinions.
Cullen Hightower

Early in my journey, it was important I learn to speak up, to articulate clearly who I was and what I felt. I had to learn how to express what I had never previously said. With maturity, I learned I don't need to say it all. Sometimes saying nothing is the best approach. As one of my beloved mentors, Bill Fifield, says, "The highest spiritual principle of all is 'shut up.'" This is the willingness and the ability to let go of the need to know *and* the need to say.

A BLANK SLATE

Everything arises out of nothing, comes out of the void, returns to the void, and goes back to nothing. All our words of the past day have disappeared. All experience arises in the present, does its dance, and disappears.
Jack Kornfield

When everything disappears, we have a Tabula Rasa, a blank slate, a new opportunity. We can see past everything we *think* we know. We can understand everything is really just our interpretation. And it doesn't mean anything except for the meaning we give it. From this place, we can actively design our lives.

> Life is like one of those flip books—it's a collection of symbols and pictures that become animated when we interact with it.

Every day we can start fresh. We can let go of our past concerns and our future expectations. Every moment we can choose our experience. Having a bad day? Start it over. Or don't. It's your choice.

WHAT ARE YOU WAITING FOR?

1. What would be possible if you were willing to let go of all you think you know?
2. How does everything that you *know* get in the way of you fully experiencing your life?

12

FINDING YOUR INNER JACK

We shall not cease from exploration
And the end of all our exploring
Will be to arrive where we started
And know the place for the first time.

T. S. Eliot

When we climb out of the boxes, we see them for what they are. When we can become willing to let go of all we thought we knew, we have a new level of freedom. And after all of that, all of our exploration, we arrive back where we started. Yet now we can see it clearly, as if for the first time.

We arrive when we let go of the limitations of the past and the fears of the future. We come full circle and we realize that what we were waiting for has been here all along. We arrive and find our inner Jack.

We no longer need to look outside ourselves for that which we already are. We no longer need to see ourselves as broken or deficient, as missing something. We are whole. We have answers. The wisdom lies within us, and now we can see and hear it. We have cleared away enough of the noise and distractions to listen and understand.

We will always explore, for it is human to explore, and change is a constant. We will arrive at places that are constantly changing, and we will land on moving targets. When we achieve a goal, we will create new ones. We will find a relationship, and then create the next level of connectedness. We will grow spiritually, and then want to go deeper.

I was always looking outside myself for strength and confidence,
but it comes from within. It is there all the time.
Anna Freud

The whole time I thought I was waiting for Jack I was really waiting for me.

I was waiting for me to stop waiting, to stop seeking, to stop searching. I realized all that wondering and wandering brought me to where I am today. After all these years, I finally accepted I will be a life-long explorer. And I can be grateful for the life I have right now.

On my refrigerator, I have a collection of quotations. Like Anna Freud's words, they provide the important (and necessary) reminder of who I really am. The truth is, if I (or any of us) really knew this, I wouldn't have been waiting for Jack. Part of being human is to forget who we are. Finding our inner Jack means realizing that wisdom is within— and also realizing that we will always be human. I *will* wait again. I will look outside myself for the answers. I will give my power away. And as soon as I am aware of this, I can come back to center and find my inner Jack.

Now I know I am complete (but I know I will forget this constantly). I no longer secretly have to hope I will find *the thing* that finally completes me (but I will still, from time to time, secretly hope). If I want to take another course, I can take another course. If I want to read another book, I can read another book. If I want to work with another mentor, I can work with another mentor. I can determine if I have stepped back on the self-help treadmill in an effort to "fix" myself. I can determine if my choice is from a place of strength and power or from a place of weakness where I think something is wrong with me or the world. I can choose to expand myself, to participate more fully in life, if for no reason other than the fact that I am able to choose.

THE HUMAN CONDITION

One of my inherited mantras (which I forget all the time) is, "Progress, not perfection." We can seek progress through practice. Practice means to improve by repeating. It doesn't mean we will get it right. (And it doesn't mean there is any "right.") Just as we will never cease exploration, we will always have a chance to practice. Life itself will give us plenty of opportunities!

Although we learn lessons, we are human, so we will forget and lapse back into old ways. Even when we practice and focus intently, we won't always stay in the moment. All we need to do is remember again and bring our awareness back to the present. We will continue to explore and search. We will catch ourselves looking outside ourselves for answers. *And it's all okay.*

> What if *this* is as good as it gets? It doesn't mean there is no room for improvement. This means we can give up trying to get somewhere. We can practice accepting it all. We can learn to embrace the human condition.

For many of us, part of the human condition is the inability to be content—a basic dissatisfaction with what is, the way *it* is, and how we are.

Our inability to be content has us fill our time with noise and activity. We keep busy to distract ourselves, to avoid experiencing our discontent, and to avoid being with ourselves.

In the play, *Waiting for Godot,* the characters spend much of their time distracting themselves from facing the fact that Godot might not arrive at all. As Samuel Beckett writes, their continual noise and banter are attempts "to hold the terrible silence at bay."

To avoid the silence, we surround ourselves with noise—both external, anything that comes from the outside world—the media, other people, honking horns, and our internal mind chatter. Frequently, the loudest noise of all is the voice of fear. It can easily drown out the calm, quiet voice of wisdom. In order to connect to our inner Jack, we must learn to slow down and quiet our busy, busy minds. Then we can distinguish which is the noise of fear and which is the voice of inner wisdom. If we observe, are aware, and practice being compassionate; if we notice instead of judging, something new and wondrous can arise.

WHAT DO YOU WANT YOUR LIFE TO BE ABOUT?

Now that you have found your inner Jack, you can choose what is next. Now that you are awake, you no longer have to wait.

> Do you know what's wrong with the world?
>
> Well, nothing is actually wrong with the world. What's "wrong" is that we *think* something is wrong, and we demonstrate this misconception through our views, our attitudes, and our positions.

Most have heard that "what you resist persists." Mother Teresa was once asked why she didn't participate in anti-war demonstrations. Her response was, "I will never do that, but as soon as you have a pro-peace rally, I'll be there." When we are opposed to something, we actually strengthen it. When we become attached and righteous, we are no longer effective. When we put our focus on what's wrong, it expands. We become part of the problem and no longer part of the solution.

What if we weren't anti-anything? What if we accepted Gandhi's invitation to be the change we want to see, regardless of the circumstances? Recently I saw a bumper sticker that said, "If you are not outraged, you aren't paying attention." I am sure the person who put this sticker on their car had good intentions, but do we really need to be outraged? And if we are *not* outraged, does that really mean we aren't paying attention? Maybe it's actually the opposite. By not being outraged, we are more present to the miracle that life is. We are more able to see effective solutions, to view positive options instead of focusing on what is wrong.

BUT I DON'T WANNA

Frequently, before I go out in the world to make a difference by speaking or leading a seminar, I don't want to go. I resist. I wonder if I am up to the task. Everything seems to be holding me back, and I find a million other things to do. Even cleaning the cat box seems compelling. I allow myself to admit that staying home in my pajamas would be so much easier, safer, and more comfortable.

We all have our methods of procrastination and avoidance when it comes to our commitments. My dear friend Talitha described, in exquisite detail, how she spent hours finding, then purchasing an antique teddy bear when what she was *supposed* to be doing was studying for her final exams. Prior to that moment, owning an antique teddy bear had *never* crossed her mind. My mother spent an entire afternoon ironing Christmas ribbons (in July) when she was attempting to finish her thesis.

Our human desire for security and safety is sneaky; it makes us want to do nothing other than be comfortable. As a result, we may not be the person we aspire to be, do the things that express our passions, or have the life we desire. If we only dwell in our comfort, the world will probably pass us by, and nothing will change. We may never become who we truly want and are intended to be.

When I catch myself going down the path of seeking comfort over my commitments, I gently remember who I am and what is important to me. My human desire for comfort doesn't have to determine how my life goes. So I breathe deeply, throw back my shoulders, hold my head high, and do what I said I would do.

We are here to awaken from the illusion of our separateness.
Thich Nhat Hanh

When we see the world from a beginner's mind, we can also see the interconnectedness of all things. We see through the illusion of separateness. We know we are part of a greater whole.

What is the meaning of life? It is what we make it mean. It is what we are committed to. We get to say what our life will be about. For some of us, it might look like a life of meditation and prayer, but for others, we are full-on expressing our humanity in the stream of life. Maybe for some it's in between. The world is full of different approaches and paths because of the vast variety in outlooks, beliefs, and values. Through our journey, along our path, we become awake. Whatever our expression, it's perfect. And whatever we choose is fine.

BE A FIERCE DISRUPTION OF THE ORDINARY

If you don't live it, it won't come out your horn.
Charlie Parker

Don't worry if you don't know what to do; you can start where you are. You can practice generosity. You can stand for something such as freedom, opportunity, equality, or love—to name just a few. Or you can create something new. Be inventive, create the unimaginable, awaken the world *or* weed your garden. No matter what the circumstance or situation, there is always the opportunity (as my dear mentor Bill always says) to "see what you can bring."

You can disrupt the ordinary by:

> Loving generously.
> Letting others be right.
> Allowing other drivers to merge before you—even when you're running late.
> Feeding the hungry in Africa.
> Feeding the hungry in your own city.
> Picking up trash at the beach.

Sending mom flowers for no particular occasion.
Helping a child do his or her homework.
Paying the bills early.
Or by taking imperfect action!

It will never be the *right* time. Possibly we will never *feel* ready. Yet, whatever we do, we can practice disrupting the ordinary by being extraordinary. We can offer people more than they expect. We can strive to do good for others without expecting rewards. We can always give our best, not because we should, but because we can.

Final Words

There's nothing to prove, nothing to figure out, nothing to get, nothing to understand. When we finally stop explaining everything to ourselves, we may discover that in silence, complete understanding was here all along.
Steve Hagen, *Buddhism Is Not What You Think*

We have arrived. We are home. We can stop trying so hard. We can stop regretting the past or fearing the future. All we have is now, and everything is okay. We realize we are whole, complete, and perfect. But we will forget *all of this*. Yet the moment we forget, we can remember again.

All is well. This is heaven on earth. It is simply perfect just the way it is and just the way it isn't. It's as good as we choose it to be at any moment, no matter what.

In the end, I discovered *we* really do know Jack.

And I am restored to wonder.

What Are You Waiting For?

1. What is the meaning of life to you?
2. What do you want your life to be about—to stand for?
3. How do you want to be remembered?
4. Who are you going to be for the world?

We were made to enjoy music, to enjoy beautiful sunsets,
to enjoy looking at the billows of the sea
and to be thrilled with a rose that is bedecked with dew …
Human beings are actually created for the transcendent,
for the sublime, for the beautiful, for the truthful … and
all of us are given the task of trying to make this world
a little more hospitable to these beautiful things.
Desmond Tutu

INTO ACTION

As I expressed in the beginning of this book, I'm not making the claim that you'll never wait again! As long as your heart is beating, you will wait. It's one of the things we humans do. In fact, you may wait a lot.

However, I have found six key principles that will propel you into action *when* you catch yourself waiting. These principles are simple, but powerful—if you use them.

The moment I felt inspired to write this book was life-altering and extraordinary. I felt fully alive, on fire! But pretty soon the doubts crept in. Some nights I cried and wanted to surrender and quit; others I celebrated my courage. I wrote, re-wrote, ripped it all up, burned what was left, and started over. I hired editors, changed directions, and then changed back. I danced in the moonlight and curled up in a ball on the floor. I told *everyone* I was writing a book, and then wished I hadn't. I grew, contracted, then grew again, stretching further than I ever thought possible. But most importantly, I lived these principles, and now I want you to have them.

Principle #1: Simple actions *can* lead to extraordinary results. When I grabbed that hundred-dollar bill out of Jack Canfield's hand, I did not realize the events that would unfold as a result. Although we may not recognize them at the time, we all have these moments where taking a simple action alters life dramatically. Commit to action when you have the opportunity—even if you are not sure of where the opportunity might lead. To paraphrase W. H. Murray, "The moment one definitely commits oneself, providence moves too."

Principle #2: Either we have a past, or it has us. Conversely to Principle #1, through a series of seemingly minor events, we may we come to know ourselves as people who stop. I call these the "Chick-a-go" moments for the time in third grade when reading out loud I said, "The Windy City is also known as Chick-a-go," and the whole class laughed. In that moment I let my past "have" me. From then on, to avoid any risk of failure or humiliation, I played it safe. I gathered evidence to add to my belief that I wasn't enough. Only later did I realize that I could choose a new interpretation. And sometimes we need to reinterpret the events of our lives over and over again.

Principle #3: Your failures can become your foundation for success. We can allow our "Chick-a-go" moments to continue to limit us and hold us back, *or* we can use them as an opportunity for transformation. These life experiences can help us see who we *really* are, of what we are capable, and allow us to contribute to others. The mythical phoenix rises from the ashes to be reborn. And from crisis we have an opportunity to create something new.

Principle #4: Inspiration is an inner phenomenon. Inspiration *can* become one more thing we seek outside ourselves. We may be inspired by something external; however the sensation actually wells up from within. It's easy to be inspired in the presence of great beauty. Who isn't inspired by the majesty of the Grand Canyon? Yet often we have such an experience then forget where the feeling originates. We can develop the muscle of generating and being responsible for our own inspiration.

Principle #5: Support inspiration with action. Inspiration is a catalyst to propel us forward to the unknown, but it won't carry us when we hit roadblocks along the way. The feeling is not enough. Taking action seems easy when we're inspired, but who are we going to be when inspiration wanes? And it will. Don't let your fleeting inspiration stop you. To sustain inspired ideas, develop an action plan and create an infrastructure.

Principle #6: Be a fierce disruption of the ordinary by honoring your commitments and embracing your humanity. As long as we are breathing, we will *never* stop being human. We will forget who we are and what we *can* do. Sometimes we will want to run and hide. Sometimes we will wait. We can live our commitments regardless and through this process discover how powerful we really are.

Life happens. Things happen. Unless we become aware, we will always be at the effect of circumstance. Simple actions *can lead* to extraordinary results. And even more amazing, this can happen in the middle of an unproductive period of waiting.

I thought the "Chick-a-go" moments were stop signs; they weren't. They were course corrections and opportunities. I still have those moments. We will *always* have those moments. There will be hundreds of opportunities to stop, and we can choose to move forward anyway.

I said I didn't have the answer for you, but if there were one, this would be it: the way to stop waiting is to embrace it. You *will* wait again. Catch yourself and accept it! We can learn to accept our humanity and love the "Chick-a-go" moments. And from there, choose to move forward.

Here's the bottom line: We are all *Waiting for Jack*—whatever or whoever "Jack" is. We falsely believe the gifts of life are just around the corner, that anywhere is better than here, that one day we will arrive and everything will be okay. So we don't try; we give up. We sell out and we forget who we are. We are afraid to succeed, afraid to fail, and afraid to say we are afraid. But as Wayne Gretzky said, "You'll always miss one-hundred percent of the shots you don't take!"

So take the shot, get on the path, and move forward. Authentically give your word to something that matters to you. And remember, you don't have to wait for Jack.

YOU DON'T HAVE TO WAIT

What are *you* waiting for? Join the movement and disrupt your ordinary.

Be heard! Share your comments, questions and stories. How did you disrupt your ordinary? What did you learn along the way? What are you creating now?

Continue this exploration with me by participating in various ways:

- Are you are a self-help junkie? Take a quick and fun quiz to find out.

- Don't know what you are passionate about? Discover how to find your passion.

- Always dreamed of writing a book? (I *know* you have a book in you.) I will help you fulfill this dream—show you how to write it and get it published.

- Want to join the movement to "Reinvent Self-Help" but don't know where to start? Learn more!

Join me in a making a profound difference in the world today.

Go to: www.waitingforjack.com/themovement

ABOUT THE AUTHOR

Kristen Moeller, MS, is a coach, speaker, author, and radio show host. She delights in "disrupting the ordinary" and inspiring others to do the same. Kristen first discovered her passion for personal development in 1989 after recovering from an eating disorder and addiction. After years of struggling with low self-esteem, she realized that recovery and joy *is* possible. Determined to provide this for others, Kristen immersed herself in the field of personal growth, earning a master's degree in mental health counseling, volunteering and working in treatment centers while continuing to train and develop herself.

After many years of serving her clients, she discovered she was ready to disrupt the ordinary once again. While reading Jack Canfield's book *The Success Principles,* she created an ambitious vision for her life. She declared her desire to challenge herself in new ways and make a difference for people on a larger scale.

Early in 2008, Kristen was inspired to write *Waiting for Jack.* Jumping into action, she began to explore our tendency to wait and what it means to be human.

In June of 2008, Kristen attended Book Expo America with 37,000 other people. Ready to propel her success to the next level, Kristen embraced the principles she shares in her book. Through a series of simple actions and her sincere commitment, she left the expo with a powerful agent, a New York publisher, and the enthusiastic support of Jack Canfield, who agreed to write the foreword to this book. By August, Kristen began her weekly internet radio show, "What Are You Waiting For?" creating a dynamic conversation with expert guests (Joan

Borysenko, Bob Doyle, Janet Attwood and Gary Goldstein, to name a few) about disrupting the ordinary and creating the *extraordinary.*

Kristen utilizes her awe-inspiring energy and motivation to bring awareness to heartfelt causes. She serves as a celebrity ambassador to the National Eating Disorder Association, and through her own non-profit, The Chick-a-go Foundation, provides "pay it forward" scholarships for people to attend transformational educational events.

Her mission for the world is that we "fiercely disrupt our ordinary," whatever the expression. Most importantly, Kristen wishes that we embrace what it means to be human—we will wait, we will seek, we will forget who we are, *and* we will remember. She wants us to know it's all okay.

When she is not actively making a difference in the world, Kristen Moeller thrives in the beauty of Colorado, playing outdoors, riding her horse or just spending time relaxing in her magical, solar powered home. She lives with two large dogs, an ornery cat, and her best friend and husband of fourteen years.

JACKNOWLEDGMENTS

My cup runneth over …

I am filled with gratitude for the people in my life. Thank you to *all* who have touched my heart, enriched my life, and made me a better person.

To my husband and best friend David—without your love and undying encouragement, I could *not* have done this. You are the love of my life, my hero and a gift to this world. You make me want to be a better woman.

To my family—Dad, Mom, Jerry, Rob, Patricia, Augustus and Tristan—for your unconditional love, support, and belief in me. Thank you Mom and Dad—for the extraordinary parenting job that you did and for the phenomenal people that you are. And a special thank you to my mother, Dotty Westby, whose exquisite drawings grace this book. Thank you for *not* waiting to return to your extraordinary talent.

To Katie and David Cottrell—for your support over the years and for giving birth to the love of my life. To the rest of the Cottrell clan, thank you for welcoming me with loving arms. To the Boyers—for your stimulating wit, tremendous intellect, and zest for life. You all have inspired me in many ways. To the Westbys—for your contribution to the world and your fantastic humor which has always cheered my soul. To J. Lea Weaver and Jessica Weaver—who overcame the horrific loss of your mother to become the beautiful people that you are.

To my "Amazing Women" group—for your commitment to the world; for cheering me on with enduring support, love and encouragement and believing in me when I forgot who I was: Dusty Meehan, Jessica Wilson, Elaina McMillan, Susan Irey, and Sheila Kelly.

To my "Girls Club"—for being powerful women and for sharing your lives and your time with me: Kristina Hall, Anne Gillespie, Ann Sparks, Robyn Thayer, Nina Faust, and Teri Winget.

To Megan Cook for never going away and for being MBFAOFITWWW since 8th grade!

To all my other powerful and gorgeous friends—words cannot describe how blessed I am to have you in my life. You have touched my heart in countless ways: Linda Gancitano, Julia and Chris Bonafede, Lynn and Laurie McHeffey, Chris, Layla, and Cassidy Meehan, Talitha and Bill Wegner, Denise McGuire, Steve Wilson, Ashley Irey, Laurie Kagan-Kark, Jenn Lofgren, Kris Samuelson, Sean Gillespie, Claudia and Marc Landau, Ron Nash, DeeDee Hirsch, Deb Berndt, Darren Jacklin, Clara Ann Chorley, Lisa Harris, Martha Runnette, Cyndi McChesney, Marny Danneberg, Juliann Cunningham, Kathleen Hart, Frank Albert, Betts Silverman, Greg Carman, Kelly Heltzel, Vicky Golder, Penny, Barry, and Brie Berman, Nancy Crivello, Jason and Kristen Champion, Maxine Champion, Cate Eaton, Amy and Andy Grant, Denye and Robbie Robbins, Dale Heckerman, Jimmy and Lisa Hutto, Linza and Eric Douglas, Bev Tuel, Jessie Loberg, Monette McIver, Krissy O'Hagin, Christie "Brooke" Otte, Heshie Segal, Rod Smith, Mark Tracey, Eileen Turpin, Stacy Karacostas, Charlie Cook, and Robert Wheaton.

To all the loving people of the Mountain Club—you know who you are! Thank you for continuing to create a place of refuge, recovery, and service.

To all my beloved mentors and coaches—for continually calling me into greatness, by raising the bar for me, showing me what is possible, and by being a fierce disruption of the ordinary. Bill and Sandy Fifield— for tirelessly shining your light and for showing me the "portals of creation." Roger Armstrong—for demanding excellence and repeatedly telling me that the only thing wrong with me is that *I think* something is wrong with me. Suzanne Levy—for your continuous love and words of wisdom. Pat Burns—for your brilliance and for insisting that I go to BEA. Janna Moll—for lovingly bringing me back to balance so many times. Lon and Sandy Golnick—for teaching me what an extraordinary relationship is. Jack Schmidt—for those early days and for the "Desiderata." Carolyn McCormick—for holding a vision for me that I didn't yet see. Susan Oliver—for your unending support during my "troubled" years. Greg Blackbourn and Dale Clarke—for your constant generosity, your patience and your assistance in getting our financial house in order.

To my hugely inspiring Platform Leaders Group—thank you Suzanne Falter-Barnes for creating the space for us and for living your message of marketing from the heart. Special thanks to Lissa and Randy Boles, Marilyn Daniels, Penny Klatell, Grace Mauzy, Anne Kirvan, Cathy Brennan, Renye Rice and Alesandra Lanto for continuing this journey together.

To the staff of Landmark Education—in particular: Sheila Wright, Jeanine Solomon, Susan Saalsa, Anne Peterson, Donna Ricardo, Abbie Weiss, Grant Lamora, and Jake Wilson—your stand for the world is breathtaking, your passion is contagious and your commitment is courageous! To the Introduction Leaders of Landmark Education (past and present), whose listening created the space for me to continue to be bigger than I thought I was—I am not going to mention you all, but please know it *is* all of you: Gail Lacroix, Mary Grace Glasier, Aria Raphael-Towner, Scott Weeden, Shannon Street, Chris Stanley, Marc Landau, Fernanda Downing, Jonathan Siegel, Erik Sale, Marie Soderberg, Dave Olsen, Casey Oberle, Rebecca Allanson, Sue Mullen, Barb Gaddy, Tara Lindis-Corbell, Angela Yost, Mark Norell, Matt Martin, Noel Wade, Laura Arbury, Kenny and Keri Blair, Belinda Lanyk, Kelly Murphy, CJ Jonca, David Brockman, Sofia Lock, Taryn

Schroeder, Tom Bruen, West Shirley, Wade and Tracie Sheppard, Will and Meg Skelton, Sharon Marcotte, and Dawn Marsh.

To all who contributed stories that are in this book—it was challenging to only be able to select a few! Thank you to those six authors of "Essays on Disrupting the Ordinary": Jessica Wilson, David Cottrell, Patricia Moeller, Gayle George, Jessica Lewis, and Dave Fichter. And thank you to those whose stories didn't go in *this* book: Chris Meehan, Marlene Chism, Dr. Philip Agrios, David Spungin, Linda Gancitano, Angel Karen Ralls, Karen Mehringer, Rick Beaver, Trish Lay, Robbie Robbins, and Margie Ahern. Thank you for taking the time to contribute your insight and experience.

To Coach Steve Toth, Nan Herring and all my co-hosts at Real Coaching Radio Network—thank you for bringing the voice of transformation to the world.

To all my clients—thank you for taking this journey with me. Thank you for your trust and for being an ongoing inspiration.

To the Law firm of Gibson, Dunn & Crutcher—for your time and dedication in setting up The Chick-a-go Foundation. Your generous contribution made the vision of the Foundation come to life.

To my trusted readers—who patiently reviewed draft after draft (after draft) and weren't afraid to give me your honest opinion, your perception, and most importantly, your precious time: Jessica Wilson, Talitha Wegner, Tara Lindis-Corbell, Alison Brush, Allison Brandt, Patricia Moeller, Chris Meehan, Suzanne Levy, Sally Ball, Kathleen Hart, Penny Berman, Bob Moeller, Dotty Westby, Laura Szabo-Cohen, and Lynn Otto.

To my editors—for taking me through different stages of this book, for teaching me about the art and craft of writing, and for contributing your vision: Hannah R. Goodman, Robin Hoffman, Kristina Hall and Mark Steisel.

To my agent, Bill Gladstone—for "recognizing" me and becoming my champion.

To Morgan James Publishing and especially Rick Frishman and David Hancock—for being great men and believing in my vision. To the Jim and Chris Howard and the design team—for your tremendous contributions. To Lyza Poulin—for taking care of me and this book in the final phase.

To the many more whose names I am not mentioning who gave me words of encouragement along the way—you may not even know the difference you made.

And ... to Jack Canfield—for being the catalyst for this book. For your generosity in writing my foreword. For the inspirational work you do and your book *The Success Principles*. For enabling me wake up and see where I wait. And for showing me that who I am *is* who I want to be!

RESOURCES

Eating Disorder Treatment and Information:
>
> The National Eating Disorder Association provides information and resources for treatment and support. *www.nationaleatingdisorders.org*
>
> Over Eaters Anonymous: a recovery program for compulsive overeating. *www.oa.org*
>
> Eating Recovery Center: A Behavioral Hospital Nourishing Health *www.EatingRecoveryCenter.com*
>
> The Renfrew Center: Residential Eating Disorder Treatment *www.RenfrewCenter.com*

Addiction Recovery:
>
> Alcoholics Anonymous: provides information on alcoholism as well questions to determine if you are an alcoholic, ways to get help, and meeting information for locations all over the world. *www.aa.org*
>
> Narcotics Anonymous: provides information on drug addiction as well questions to determine if you are a drug addict, ways to get help, and meeting information for locations all over the world. *www.na.org*

Financial Issues:
>
> Debtors Anonymous: A recovery program for people with money problems and compulsive debt. *www.debtorsanonymous.org*

The Accredited Network:

> Dale Clarke has a well-earned reputation for being the "Cash Flow Analysis Guru" by methodically finding the "leaks" in clients' incomes so that they can be plugged up and turned into production. *www.fireyourfinacialadviser.com*

> Greg Blackbourn is president of President of The Accredited Network. After more than a decade of experience in the financial services industry, he bridges the gap of Mental, Relationship, and Financial Capital. *www.gregblackbourn.com*

Best Musical Experience:

> Face Vocal Band: worth a trip to Denver—or find them online! One of my "peak experiences" mentioned in Chapter Eleven. *www.facevocalband.com*

Favorite Books:

> Attwood, Chris and Attwood, Janet Bray. *The Passion Test.* New York: Penguin Group (USA) Inc., 2008

> Canfield, Jack. *The Success Principles.* New York: HarperCollins Publishers Inc., 2005

> Chodron, Pema. *When Things Fall Apart.* Boston: Shambala Publications, Inc., 1997

> Epstein, Mark. *Going on Being.* New York: Random House, Inc., 2001

> Gilbert, Elizabeth. *Eat, Pray, Love.* New York: Penguin Group (USA) Inc; 2006

> Grogan, John. *Marley & Me.* New York: HarperCollins Publishers, 2005

Gunderson, Garrett B. *Killing Sacred Cows*. Austin: Greenleaf Book Group, LLC., 2008

Hagen, Steve. *Buddhism: Is Not What You Think*. New York: HarperCollins Publishers Inc., 2003

Hancock, David and Jay Conrad Levinson. *The Entrepreneurial Author*. New York: Morgan James Publishing, 2009

Houston, Pam. *Sight Hound*. New York: W.W. Norton & Company, Inc., 2005

Johnson, MD, Spencer. *The Precious Present*. New York: Doubleday, 1981

Kornfield, Jack. *After the Ecstasy, the Laundry*. New York: Bantam Books, 2000

Lamott, Anne. *Bird by Bird*. New York: Random House, Inc. 1994

McDonnell, Patrick. *The Gift of Nothing*. New York: Time Warner Book Group, 2005

Mortenson, Greg and Relin, David Oliver. *Three Cups of Tea*. London: Penguin Books Ltd., 2006

Tipping, Colin C. *Radical Forgiveness*. Marietta: Global 13 Publications, Inc., 2002

Tolle, Eckhart. *The Power of Now*. Novato: New World Library, 1999

10% of the author's proceeds from the sale of this book go to the Chick-a-go Foundation. The Chick-a-go Foundation is a not-for-profit organization dedicated to providing 'pay-it-forward' scholarships for people to attend transformational, life-altering educational programs.
www.chickagofoundation.org

BUY A SHARE OF THE FUTURE IN YOUR COMMUNITY

These certificates make great holiday, graduation and birthday gifts that can be personalized with the recipient's name. The cost of one S.H.A.R.E. or one square foot is $54.17. The personalized certificate is suitable for framing and will state the number of shares purchased and the amount of each share, as well as the recipient's name. The home that you participate in "building" will last for many years and will continue to grow in value.

Here is a sample SHARE certificate:

HABITAT FOR HUMANITY

THIS CERTIFIES THAT

YOUR NAME HERE

HAS INVESTED IN A HOME FOR A DESERVING FAMILY

1985-2005

TWENTY YEARS OF BUILDING FUTURES IN OUR
COMMUNITY ONE HOME AT A TIME

1200 SQUARE FOOT HOUSE @ $65,000 = $54.17 PER SQUARE FOOT
This certificate represents a tax deductible donation. It has no cash value.

YES, I WOULD LIKE TO HELP!

I support the work that Habitat for Humanity does and I want to be part of the excitement! As a donor, I will receive periodic updates on your construction activities but, more importantly, I know my gift will help a family in our community realize the dream of homeownership. **I would like to SHARE in your efforts against substandard housing in my community!** *(Please print below)*

PLEASE SEND ME _____ SHARES at $54.17 EACH = $ $_____

In Honor Of: _____

Occasion: (Circle One)   HOLIDAY   BIRTHDAY   ANNIVERSARY

        OTHER: _____

Address of Recipient: _____

Gift From: _____ *Donor Address:* _____

Donor Email: _____

I AM ENCLOSING A CHECK FOR $ $_____ PAYABLE TO HABITAT FOR HUMANITY OR PLEASE CHARGE MY VISA OR MASTERCARD *(CIRCLE ONE)*

Card Number _____ Expiration Date: _____

Name as it appears on Credit Card _____ Charge Amount $ _____

Signature _____

Billing Address _____

Telephone # Day _____ Eve _____

PLEASE NOTE: Your contribution is tax-deductible to the fullest extent allowed by law.
Habitat for Humanity • P.O. Box 1443 • Newport News, VA 23601 • 757-596-5553
www.HelpHabitatforHumanity.org